Secondary English
Planning for Learning in the Classroom

Nicholas McGuinn
and
Nicola Onyett

W0006500

continuum

Continuum International Publishing Group

The Tower Building	80 Maiden Lane
11 York Road	Suite 704
London SE1 7NX	New York, NY 10038

www.continuumbooks.com

British Library Cataloguing-in-Publication Data
A catalogue record for this book is available from the British Library.

ISBN: 978-1-4411-4313-6 (paperback)
ISBN: 978-0-8264-3345-9 (hardcover)

Library of Congress Cataloging-in-Publication Data
McGuinn, Nicholas.
  Secondary English : planning for learning in the classroom / Nicholas McGuinn and Nicola Onyett.
    p. cm.
  ISBN 978-0-8264-3345-9 (hardcover)
  ISBN 978-1-4411-4313-6 (pbk.)
  1. English language–Rhetoric–Study and teaching. 2. English literature–Study and teaching (Secondary) 3. English language–Study and teaching (Secondary) 4. English literature–Study and teaching (Secondary) 5. Literacy–Study and teaching (Secondary) I. Onyett, Nicola, 1966- II. Title.

LB1632.M355 2010
428.0071'2–dc22

2010015144

Typeset by Newgen Imaging Systems Pvt Ltd, Chennai, India
Printed and bound in India by Replika Press Pvt Ltd

Contents

Introduction

Anybody interested in reading about the nature and practice of English teaching already has plenty of good material from which to choose. Why then do we need another book on the subject? Most books designed for people thinking about training to teach English are concerned with identifying its skills and its content and then with suggesting innovative and engaging ways in which the skills and the content might be taught. This is an understandable approach: what we might define as 'subject English' has grown dramatically in the recent past so that it now transcends traditional boundaries of language and literature to incorporate communication modes and texts of all kinds. Keeping abreast of these developments is a task in itself and one which needs constant monitoring and revision. Added to this is the fact that, in the United Kingdom certainly and in other parts of the English-speaking world probably too, government initiatives mean that the curriculum and its accompanying assessment procedures are subject to regular change.

Amidst all this change, however, certain things remain constant. Whether recording a podcast, posting a blog on a virtual learning environment, or writing on a blackboard with a piece of chalk, there are fundamental and generic pedagogical issues with which all English teachers need to engage. Good as they are about telling us how we might teach Shakespeare or encourage different forms of writing, we feel that other books are less accommodating to these core issues. This is why, rather than provide yet another review of the four modalities of English or the teaching of grammar or the place of literature and drama in the curriculum, we have chosen to base our book upon five key areas of pedagogical concern: *differentiation, emotional intelligence, ways of learning, thinking skills* and *assessment*. As trainers of secondary English teachers, we find that our students are very good at devising exciting and imaginative ideas for engaging with poetry or novels or the media; but they feel less secure about how to plan for focussed, purposeful learning in the classroom so that these five key areas are given their due.

We decided to write this book because we wanted to address in writing these perennial issues which arise year after year in our English method university classrooms. We ask our trainees to consider two core questions: *What will your students learn in your lesson and how will you know that the learning has taken place?* These two questions are fundamental to our practice and each of our five chapters attempts to show how we might identify and address the complex issues which those two seemingly simple questions raise. You will not, therefore, find in this book a chapter on reading or speaking and listening or grammar or information and communications technology and so on. What you will find are a series of case studies of oral and written texts created by students we have encountered during our careers with associated key questions and reflection activities designed to help you engage with the process of careful, focussed assessment which we believe is the starting point for all good planning and teaching. We explore, therefore, the issues raised by each case study and build on this exploration to try to find ways of advancing the learning of each of the students concerned.

We try to engage in dialogue with each other across the chapters, just as we do on a regular basis in our method work at the University of York. As you engage with that dialogue, you will encounter certain thinkers about education who have helped to shape our ideas over the years. Thus, Bruner, De Corte and Vygotsky feature heavily throughout the book. Bloom's Taxonomy – particularly in its updated twenty-first-century manifestation – provides important guidance to us in, for example, Chapters 4 and 5. The *seven levels of the writing code* template is applied to the writing of two 11-year olds in Chapter 1 and again to the work of a 14-year-old in Chapter 3. In the first instance, the template serves to illuminate the zone of proximal development within the context of differentiation. In the second case, it is used to explore issues relating to learning styles. To take another example, issues regarding the encouragement of powerful talk in the classroom are investigated in Chapter 4 and then an example of such talk is subjected to close analysis in Chapter 5.

Having begun this introduction by describing how this work is not meant to be like most other books about learning to teach English, it is important to emphasize that its concerns are very firmly located within the subject we both love and to which we have dedicated our professional lives. You will find references to writing, to Shakespeare, to Dickens, to contemporary authors like David Almond, or Lorna Sage or Geoffrey Hill, to the wealth of new technologies which have so radically changed the way we think about text and communication, to the various models of pedagogy which have informed the practice of English teachers over the centuries. However, what lies at the heart of this book are individual learners who are struggling to become, as the poet WS Graham so memorably puts it, 'alive in the language': there are Mark and Natalie, for example, doing their first piece of writing for their English teacher at 'big school'; there is Melanie, talking to her class mates about a very severe medical procedure which she had to undergo; there is Asif, choosing to write about the sudden death of his little brother; and there is Lucy, afraid that she might embarrass herself by saying something inappropriate in her senior literature seminar. If we keep the thought of those very different individuals in our minds as we plan for learning in the English classroom, we cannot fail to appreciate what an important enterprise we are engaged in.

Nicholas McGuinn
Nicola Onyett
University of York 2010

1 Differentiation

Chapter Outline

Key Questions

The following key questions underpin the chapter:

1. Can a case be made against differentiation?
2. Is differentiation by outcome an adequate response?
3. Should boys and girls be taught separately?
4. What other differentiation strategies are available to us?
5. Is it possible to differentiate and stay sane?
6. Is it possible to teach students of widely different abilities and needs together?

Case Study: Mark and Natalie join Year 7 in their new school

Imagine this scene. It is the first day of a new academic year. You are facing a class of thirty 11-year olds who are just about to begin their secondary school careers. The policy in your school dictates that every new pupil has to complete a timed

⇨

written assignment when they arrive, so that their new teachers can get an initial impression of the writing skills which they bring with them from primary school.

These are the instructions given to the children:

'Write a story which begins with these words: *When I looked over the wall, I couldn't believe my eyes!'*

Here are responses to that task written by two of the pupils, who, for the purposes of this book, are called Mark and Natalie:

A different world

When I looked over the wall I could hardly belive my eyes!

It was like another world, there were Castles, big glittery ones. There was also this huge tree that had big juicy apples. The huge giant was running around with the little elfs The grass was covered in lovely flowers But, the giant spotted me, I thought oh no! The Smile on the giants face disapered.
He came running over........
"Do you want to join us". Phew!
I thought he was going to eat me!

I played there all day, I looked at my watch it was still the same time as I came in." The giant said "Here the clocks stay so we have more time to play, the clocks at only changes when it becomes nine o clock then we all go. "Anyway I better go, my Mum will be worry about me"

Well I slept that night, and everyday I went, it was the best thing that happened to me!
I take all of my friends there, and they love it too!

When I looked over the wall I could hardly believe my eyes, I saw one of my friend and his name wes Dan, he work over to me and he sed "hollw" so I sed the same. We went to the park and playld football on the feald

What differentiation issues are raised by these two pieces of Year 7 writing?

Reflection Activity 1.1

What is your response to these two scripts? What are the implications for your classroom practice? How might the teacher who received these two widely differing pieces of work have liaised with colleagues across the educational phases to prevent such 'surprises' occurring in the first lesson at a new school?

Differentiation: some issues

The briefest of appraisals reveals that these two responses – stimulated by the same prompt – are significantly different from each other. How is it that a boy and a girl (can you tell who wrote which piece?) of the same age, who have been through the same national curriculum and probably the same primary school experience together, can produce work of such contrasting content and quality? These are important, challenging questions whose exploration would oblige us to face uncomfortable truths about the ways in which what Pierre Bourdieu calls 'cultural capital' is distributed in our society.

I hope it does not seem like equivocation to suggest that it is not the purpose of this chapter to seek answers to those questions. This is not for one moment to suggest that those questions are not important. You may well have chosen to be a teacher of English because you have a particular vision of what a compassionate, pluralistic, literate society might be like. You might well feel upset and angry even to think that, at such a young age, life chances appear to be hardening so depressingly along established lines of wealth and privilege.

Perhaps, however, the route to the New Jerusalem begins with the recognition that each of the children in front of you has produced a response to the assignment equally diverse as those written by Mark and Natalie. As their teachers, we owe it to the children to try to *differentiate* our practice by finding ways of meeting the learning challenges posed by those 30 individual young writers. It is a daunting prospect – as Vermunt will suggest in Chapter 3 – and at such moments, we might try to steady ourselves by thinking of the four questions which Jonothan Neelands advises teachers to consider when they embark on a new encounter with a group of students:

> What's possible for me?
> With this group?
> In this space?
> In the time I have available? (Neelands 1984: 9)

There are several ways of interpreting Neelands' use of the word 'possible' here. We could read it as an example of world-weary pragmatism: it is too difficult to cater for the diverse learning needs of 30 individual writers so we are not even going to try. The National Foundation for Educational Research (NFER) team which explored teachers' perceptions of differentiation towards the close of the twentieth century found something akin to this attitude. The team noted in their report:

Behind the comments and explanations given by many teachers seemed to lie a rather wistful recognition that differentiation was an ideal which fitted their educational aims but which in practice could never be implemented in real classrooms. (Weston *et al.* 1998: 152)

To confess frankly that the task of differentiation is too difficult even to attempt might be a bleak response but it is at least an honest one. The alternative and more equivocal answer – the one often used by English teachers when we were first challenged to think about differentiation 20 years ago – would be to suggest that we 'deal with' the issue by differentiating through *outcome*.

Differentiation by outcome?

This response can be described as equivocal because it is possible to make a case for differentiation by outcome. Paradoxically, educationalists committed to equality of opportunity and provision at the height of the comprehensive movement in the United Kingdom feared that differentiation implied, as Brian Simon put it, 'the imposition of different curricula for different groups' (Simon 1985: 4). Certain privileged pupils would get an enriched curriculum and others would not. Susan Hart expresses the dilemma well:

I had problems in coming to terms with the emergence of 'differentiation' as a new discourse of 'good practice' because all my thinking about teaching and learning, throughout my professional life, had been developed within a framework which identified 'differentiation' not as a solution but as a major cause of inequality and under-achievement. (Hart 1996: 10)

Recalling his year as an English teacher at an intermediate (secondary modern) school on the Ballymurphy estate in Belfast in 1962, the poet Seamus Heaney witnessed the effects of such 'inequality' at first hand:

What happened was not what was supposed to happen. There was supposed to be a swerve away from the exam culture, a development of skills, an inculcation of self-respect by giving the non-academic pupils a prospect of fulfilment in other areas. But what actually happened was that the effort went into helping the top streams, the top fifth or quarter of the intake, say, to catch up in the academic race. . . . So instead of a school where equal attention was paid to all abilities, there was this favoured upper stream and then the great non-academic

> flow-through. . . . I had a PE class with a group of really low-ability first years, 1G,
> for God's sake, in a ranking that began with 1A. (O'Driscoll 2008: 69–70)

To these concerns, teachers of English might add another: the apprehension that differentiation as Simon perceives it would lead to the 'imposition' of different reading experiences – particularly of literary texts – upon different groups of pupils. Two core principles would thus be compromised: that all literature should be available to all pupils and that we create communities through shared experience. Differentiation by outcome could, viewed from this perspective, be regarded as the option which poses the least threat to such principles in that it allows all pupils to access the same text and to experience the same task together.

If we take this line, we have to live with some difficult consequences. The writing task with which this chapter opens is a classic example of differentiation by outcome in the English classroom. What has it shown us? That Natalie (you probably guessed that the first example was written by a girl) is a far more secure writer than Mark. More pertinently, we might ask, what has the task shown Natalie and Mark? Probably nothing that they did not know before: Natalie is 'good at' writing and enjoys it; Mark is not and does not. Welcome to secondary school!

Thinking about Mark's work here brings to mind the opening lines of Donald Graves' famous text *Writing: Teachers and Children at Work*:

> Children want to write. They want to write the first day they attend school. This
> is no accident. Before they went to school they marked up walls, pavements,
> newspapers with crayons, chalk, pens or pencils . . . anything that makes a mark.
> The child's marks say, 'I am.' (Graves 1983: 3)

If what Graves says here is true, then what has happened to Mark's sense of himself as a writer (and as a human being) between the day he first entered school to the moment he arrived in our class and presented us with the piece of writing shown above? That is another of the big questions; and again we might turn to Neelands' sense of the possible to help us focus on the immediate challenge. Mark is, for better or worse, our responsibility now. What can we do, in this space, in the time available – and if we actually calculate the amount of time allocated to English lessons during a school year, it is not very much – to help Mark recapture what Graves calls 'the joy of discovery' (Graves 1983: 3) in writing?

Reflection Activity 1.2

Where do you stand on the issue of differentiation? Do you feel that differentiation by outcome is an adequate response? Discuss the issue with experienced colleagues within your department and your school. How do they approach issues of differentiation? Ask them to talk you through their lesson planning process and consider together how we might plan practically for differentiation within the classroom.

We have to find a more effective and empowering strategy than differentiation by outcome. To subject Mark to more writing tasks like the one which opens this chapter is to offer him nothing but a bleak sequence of opportunities to reveal his own insecurities as a writer and to ponder the gap in development between his work and Natalie's. And what will Natalie gain from the process? She too risks becoming trapped in a cycle. How many times does she need to prove that she has come to secondary school equipped with more secure writing skills than Mark? How will this help her aspire or develop? In such circumstances, the temptation for both students to disengage from their school experience would be strong and understandable.

There is another way of interpreting Neelands' concept of the possible: the interpretation implicit in the title of Jerome Bruner's *Actual Minds, Possible Worlds*. Bruner writes about the empowerment which can come from the act of 'subjunctivizing reality' by focussing upon the imaginative potential of verbs like *could, might, would, should*. As Bruner puts it:

> To be in the subjunctive mode is . . . to be trafficking in human possibilities rather than in settled certainties. (Bruner 1986: 26)

The American psychologist Urie Bronfenbrenner proposed an *Ecological Systems Theory* which suggested that learning takes place within four types of 'nested systems'. These 'circle outwards' from the individual – like four increasingly wide ripples from the centre of a pond – in a movement from *microsystem* (the family or classroom, for example) to the *macrosystem* (the larger socio-cultural context within which individuals live out their lives) (Bronfenbrenner: 1979).

Differentiation by gender?

One way in which we might differentiate on a microsystemic level could be to separate Mark and Natalie's cohort into two single sex groups. This is a policy which has been explored and evaluated in a number of United Kingdom schools recently, nor least because of concerns about the persistent gap in performance between the sexes, particularly in English. The difference in standard between the writing of Mark and Natalie is reflected nationwide amongst 11-year-olds. Reviewing national test data over an eight-year period for the *Raising Boys' Achievement Project* in 2005, the report team notes:

> national data over the period 1996–2004 reveal that although there has been little difference between the percentages of boys and girls achieving level 4 or above in the National Curriculum key stage 2 . . . tests in Mathematics and Science, there has been a marked disparity between the attainment of boys and girls in English. Here, girls have persistently outperformed boys in both reading and writing. (Younger and Warrington 2005: 20)

Judging from the national data, the prognosis for Mark as he moves through the various stages of secondary education becomes bleaker still:

> This gender gap persists and widens in the secondary school context. When girls and boys are tested at the age of 14, at the end of key stage 3, for example, there is frequently around a 15 percentage point difference commonly recorded in achievement levels at National Curriculum Level 5(+) in English and in many of the Humanities, Languages and Creative Arts subjects, although again the difference in mathematics and science is much smaller. . . .
>
> The academic attainments of boys and girls in their GCSE examinations, taken at the end of compulsory schooling at the age of 16, reveal similar patterns of disparity at school, local education authority and national level. (Younger and Warrington 2005: 21)

Four years further on, estimates of 2008 national examination results for 14-year-olds suggested little improvement. The percentage of boys achieving Level 5 in both English and mathematics was provisionally assessed at 62% compared with 71% of girls (DCSF 2008: 16). Drawing upon evidence taken from more than 50 primary, secondary and special schools in England between 2000 and 2004, the authors of the *Raising Boys' Achievement Project* suggest that:

> Evidence in favour of the development of single-sex classes for some subjects,
> from both students' voices and from an analysis of levels of academic achievement,
> is nonetheless persuasive. (Younger and Warrington 2005: 13)

The report notes that single-sex classes appeared to enhance the achievement of girls in Maths and Science and – particularly interesting for our purposes – boys in English. Examples of good practice in the latter cited by the authors include: provision of a rich range of textual experiences; paired reading schemes; a variety of sharply focused, well-paced learning activities including opportunities for Drama. Above all, the authors emphasize the centrality of purposeful, collaborative talk as a way into productive reading and writing.

It is possible to argue that single sex groupings might allow students to engage more effectively with each of these strategies – particularly during the complex, self-conscious years of adolescence. Teachers working with single sex groups could construct a reading curriculum designed specifically for the perceived needs and interests of boys or girls; students, for their part, might feel less inhibited about participating in Drama and discussion or sharing their concerns about reading and writing if their collaborators were exclusively members of the same sex. Consider the evidence taken from an email mentoring project designed to link under-achieving 14-year-old boys from two different schools, one in the north and one in the south of England. Their brief was to support each other by email exchange as they worked with their individual teachers on George Orwell's novel *Animal Farm*. After a few opening salvoes of bluster and boasting (mainly about the relative merits of different football teams) the boys' discourse changed. It became more reflective and academically focussed, even ranging into a discussion of texts beyond the specific brief of the project:

> So what work are you doing at the moment? We are doing Shakespeare, and
> I really like it. . . . The topic that we are doing on Shakespeare is *Julius Caesar.*

The boys offered progress reports on their engagement with *Animal Farm* and other work in English lessons and they made gestures of support for each other's work:

> We have done are [sic] leaflets [for an exercise on persuasive writing] and we are
> reading animal farm and we are up to chapter 8. I like your speech in the style of
> squealer [a character from the novel].

There were even admissions of academic insecurity:

> I can't really read some of the difficult words because I am not used to the spellings [in Shakespeare's *Julius Caesar*].

Writing in role as characters from the novel appealing for the exiled leader, Snowball, to return to save Animal Farm, the boys conveyed emotion and a sense of urgency:

> All of us wish you would come back. Animal Farm is in deep danger. (McGuinn 2001: 91–2)

At the other end of the age and ability range, here is a small A Level Literature group. The students are all girls; and you might wish to bear this extract in mind when you analyse a similar, more sustained all-girls' discussion of *A Winter's Tale* in Chapter 5. The participants in this example are exploring a cloze exercise based on Thomas Hardy's poem *When I Set Out for Lyonnesse*. In the extract shown below, the girls are trying to puzzle out what word might complete the third line of the poem. The complete version runs:

> *When I set out for Lyonnesse,*
> *A hundred miles away,*
> *The rime was on the spray,*

The printed words of a transcript cannot alone convey the atmosphere of security and engagement which prevailed as the girls pored over the text together. When you read this brief extract, you will have to imagine laughter, excitement, voices raised in mock protest as different contributors finish each other's sentences or experiment with new ideas:

Pupil A: So we still haven't got . . .
Pupil B: 'The rime was on the way
The rime was on the . . .'
Pupil C: Spey?
Pupil D: Shall we put 'Spey'?
Pupil B: Why put 'Spey'? Because 'Spey' is a river and you don't get rime on a river – you get ice.
Pupil A: No, you do! You do when it's iced over . . .
Pupil B: 'The rime was on the . . .
Pupil C: . . . 'hay'
Pupil D: You *can* get it on hay.
Pupil B: Oh yes, because it's like spiders' webs!

These two extracts certainly present English teachers with food for thought: would either the 14-year-old boys or the 17-year-old girls have used language so productively and generously if they had been working in mixed sex groups? Are single sex classrooms the answer to Mark and Natalie's individual learning needs? The authors of the *Raising Boys' Achievement* report issue a number of caveats:

> As with other intervention strategies, however, there is the need for some caution in any analysis. Such single-sex classes are not a panacea in themselves; in some schools, boys'-only classes have become very challenging to teach, or stereotyping of expectation has established a macho regime which has alienated some boys. Even in the most successful schools, both boys and girls have consistently said that they do not want to be in single-sex classes for *all* lessons. (Younger and Warrington 2005: 13)

The point about 'stereotyping of expectations' is particularly significant here. Would *all* 11-year-old girls respond to the story writing brief at the start of this chapter in the way that Natalie does? Would *all* 11-year-old boys produce work like Mark's? If girls are significantly out performing boys, does this mean that all girls are doing well in English and all boys are doing badly? What other variables – ethnicity or class, for example – might be at work here? When the *Raising Boys' Achievement* team teased out the Key Stage 2 Performance Profiles of the 11-year-olds who took national tests between 1996 and 2004, they noted interesting gender variations in performance across the modalities of English, as this example from 2004 indicates:

Table 1.1 Percentage of boys and girls achieving level 4 or above in national tests (2004)

English	Boys	Girls
Overall score	72	83
Reading	79	87
Writing	56	71

(Adopted from Younger and Warrington 2005: 22)

Girls might be consistently out-performing boys here; but this does not mean that theirs is a story of all-round success. 29% of them, for example, failed to achieve a Level 4 in Writing – and this must be a concern, even if the number of underachievers is far less than that for the boys in the same cohort.

Planning for differentiation: the zone of proximal development

Clearly, if we are to differentiate effectively, we need something more nuanced than the broad-brush approach of single sex groupings. This is where we might turn to Lev Vygotsky for a third interpretation of the word 'possible'. One of the most important contributions that Vygotsky made to our thinking was to shift the focus of assessment from the measurement of what students can actually do to what, with guidance, they have the *potential* to achieve:

> Most of the psychological investigations concerned with school learning measured the level of mental development of the child by making him solve certain standardized problems. The problems he was able to solve by himself were supposed to indicate the level of his mental development at the particular time. But in this way, only the completed part of the child's development can be measured, which is far from the whole story. We tried a different approach. Having found that the mental age of two children was, let us say, eight, we gave each of them harder problems than he could manage on his own and provided some slight assistance: the first step in a solution, a leading question, or some other form of help. We discovered that one child could, in cooperation, solve problems designed for twelve-year-olds, while the other could not go beyond problems intended for nine-year-olds. (Vygotsky 1986: 187)

This is a long quotation from one of Vygotsky's seminal texts, *Thought and Language*; but it is particularly important to this chapter for two reasons. First, it reinforces the impression created by the writing of Mark and Natalie: pupils of the same age can be at very different stages of development. In Vygotsky's words, 'mental age' is not a particularly helpful guide to 'the dynamics of intellectual progress' (Vygotsky 1986: 187). Second – and this is where the word 'possible' is particularly pertinent – it affirms the purpose and the value of the teacher by asserting that children can achieve more – sometimes dramatically more – with authoritative guidance than they can on their own (and again, you might want to bear this point in mind when you analyse the role of the teacher in the *Winter's Tale* discussion transcript reproduced in Chapter 5). One of Vygotsky's many important legacies to us is the concept of the 'zone of proximal development' which he defines pithily as

> The discrepancy between a child's actual mental age and the level he reaches in solving problems with assistance . . . (Vygotsky 1986: 187)

Despite what Vygotsky says here about the uneasy relationship between mental age and intellectual development, the school that Mark and Natalie attend – typically of schools throughout the United Kingdom – groups its pupils chronologically. If we are to differentiate effectively for Mark, Natalie and the other 28 members of the class, we need to establish their zones of proximal development so that we can help them realize their potential as learners.

The uses and limits of data

Thanks to advances in technology, we have, here in England, a wealth of data to help us begin this process. Like the members of the *Raising Boys' Achievement* team quoted above, we can make use of examination statistics, accessing sophisticated information on-line which enables us to compare results and identify trends over time at a national, local authority and school level. We have already considered some of the gender issues yielded by this information; but we might also wish to consider how Mark and Natalie's examination results compare with those of pupils from schools in similar – or even very dissimilar – socio-economic areas. Thinking of Bronfenbrenner again and moving to a *macrosystemic* level, we might draw upon the resources provided by the *International Association for the Evaluation of Educational Achievement* (IEA) and access the *Progress in International Reading Literacy Study* (PIRLS) website http://www.pirls.org to consider how students here have measured up across the three investigative cycles (2001, 2006 and 2011) in comparison with their international counterparts. If we want more information about the English perspective, we can access the report on the 2006 cycle written by a team from the *National Foundation for Educational Research* (NFER) (Twist et al. 2007) www.nfer.ac.uk/pirls Ranging back down through Bronfenbrenner's 'nested systems', we might consult the Fischer Family Trust data, http://www.fischertrust.org for Mark and Natalie's year group. This could help us to estimate the progress they are likely to make during their secondary school careers and to fine-tune any targets we might wish to set them so that we can try to take account of some of those performance variables mentioned earlier in the chapter.

All of this information (most, you will notice, available at the click of a computer mouse) is immensely powerful. If used sensitively and insightfully, it can help teachers make authoritative, informed decisions about the differentiated learning needs of the individual students in their care. However, figures need to be treated with caution because they have a tendency to assume a life of their own. Taking the nomenclature of the current English system as an example, there is a danger that we might declare that a student is working at

Level 3 (for instance) in the modality of writing without really thinking through what that actually means in terms of individual writers' ability to, in Arnold's telling phrase, develop 'their own capacity to make a mark in the world' (1991: 32). The philosopher John Locke alerted us to the problem several centuries ago:

> when we would consider, or make propositions about . . . more complex ideas, as of a *man, vitriol, fortitude, glory,* we usually put the name for the idea: because the ideas these names stand for, being for the most part imperfect, confused, and undetermined, we reflect on the names themselves, because they are more clear, certain, and distinct, and readier occur to our thoughts than the pure ideas: and so we make use of these words instead of the ideas themselves, even when we would meditate and reason within ourselves, and make tacit mental propositions.
> (Canfield and Donnell 1964: 258)

If we are to locate Mark and Natalie's respective zones of proximal writing development we need to keep those 'clear, certain, and distinct' National Curriculum Levels – helpful though they might be – in perspective. We need to focus upon the 'imperfect, confused, and undetermined' actualities revealed in the written work my new pupils have placed before us. Geoff Petty argues that all topics can be explored from two, equally necessary, analytical perspectives: the 'atomistic' and the 'holistic'. He represents the former with the metaphor of a knife and the latter with that of a pair of spectacles. The holistic perspective, Petty continues, allows the viewer to 'look at the *whole* from *different points of view*' [Petty's italics] (Petty 2006: 326). The start of this chapter suggested some of the 'lenses' – to continue Petty's metaphor – which might be applied to Mark and Natalie's work (and to their situation as human beings). The holistic approach is of course crucial to the nurturing of writers. Summarizing the research into the development of written language in 7 to 14 year-olds undertaken by Wilkinson and others during the 1970s (Wilkinson et al. 1980), Richard Andrews emphasizes the importance of their conclusion that teachers need to 'take into account such factors as the emotional, moral and cognitive development of the children behind the texts' (Andrews 2001: 58). Work like this takes time and patience. As relationships develop, teacher and student can establish the sense of trust and understanding necessary for purposeful communication. Time and patience are vital, too, for the implementation of those positive strategies recommended by practitioners of the art: engaging in dialogue; modelling; interviewing; conferencing; providing real contexts, purposes and audiences for writing; establishing a school ethos in which the written word and its creators (at all levels of ability) are celebrated within and beyond the classroom (Andrews 2001, Graves 1983, OFSTED 2003).

Wielding the assessment 'knife'

This is for later. Our immediate need is to take the 'atomistic' approach and, as Petty puts it, to 'cut up the topic into discrete bits and look at these one at a time' (Petty 2006: 326). The knife metaphor is useful because it evokes a scalpel's forensic application. This is perhaps an unusual analogy for a teacher to make: so much of our work is located within the affective domain. We invest so much of ourselves, our sense of identity, our values, our passions, in our teaching. Sometimes, however, if we are really going to help our students, we need the clear-sighted, professional detachment of the surgeon. We need a systematic procedure which will allow us to analyse the evidence presented by Mark and Natalie so that we can use this to, in Bruner's words, 'subjunctivize reality' for them and then start to deal in 'human possibilities'.

One useful taxonomy to apply in this context is Andrews' model of the writing code, because it allows both the forensic analysis suggested by the knife image and the holistic application of Petty's 'spectacles'. Working from the *grapho-phonemic* to the *contextual,* Andrews suggests that written texts can be explored at each of seven incrementally more expansive levels:

1. Grapho-phonemic (sound/letter relationships)
2. Morphological (parts of words)
3. Lexical (words themselves)
4. Syntactic (phrases, clauses, sentences)
5. Sub-textual (paragraphs, stanzas)
6. Textual (whole works)
7. Contextual (historical, linguistic, generic, socio-political contexts). (Adopted from Andrews 2001: 61–2)

Andrews suggests that teachers need to distinguish between 'composition' and 'secretarial' skills (2001: 59) when engaging with students' writing. If we map Natalie's piece of work against the taxonomy (both stories are presented at the start of the chapter), we can find plentiful evidence of potential for development in both areas. Exploring the lexical level, for example, we might note her confident use of adjectives for compositional effect in the fourth line of the story where she post modifies her initial description of the other world beyond the wall:

there were castles, big glittery ones.

Secretarially, too, Natalie's lexis is secure in terms of spelling: homophone choices are selected accurately ('there', 'too') and silent letters are negotiated confidently ('lovely', 'castles', 'watch'). Applying the morphological 'spectacle', we notice that she seems to understand how to use suffixes ('running', 'covered'). Even the misspelling of 'disappeared' (she writes *disapered*) is a source of developmental potential because it indicates that Natalie is not afraid to attempt difficult words – and to do so according to logical spelling and morphological patterns which she has clearly absorbed. Application of the syntactical and sub-textual 'spectacles' reveals a use of secretarial skills to enhance compositional effect: staccato phrases and sentences, the introduction of dialogue and commentary, the liberal use of exclamation marks, even the capitalization of 'phew!' – all suggest a voice which is enthusiastic, confident and engaged with the act of writing.

The most exciting glimpse of Natalie's potential as a writer is revealed when we move to the sixth level of the writing code and consider the piece as a whole. Clearly, she possesses some understanding of narrative structure: the story sets a scene (the other world), introduces a problem (a giant looks as if he means to cause trouble for an interloper), resolves it (the giant becomes a friend) and moves to a resolution (the protagonist goes home to bed). So far, so (perhaps) unremarkable. Reading Natalie's work, however, might bring to mind two comments from Janet H Murray's fascinating book *Hamlet on the Holodeck: The Future of Narrative in Cyberspace*. Writing about the impact of visual and digital media upon our perception of narrative, Murray, using a phrase which echoes the quotation from Bruner cited earlier in this chapter, observes:

> To be alive in the twentieth century is to be aware of . . . alternative possible selves, of alternative possible worlds, and of the limitless intersecting stories of the actual world. (1997: 38)

Natalie wrote her story under timed pressure sitting in an unfamiliar classroom surrounded by new classmates together for the first time in a new school. The only prompt she was given was to imagine something remarkable when she looked over a wall. How easily, from such unpromising beginnings, she was able to construct 'an alternative possible world' populated by giants and elves, one in which time is frozen until a particular moment in each day and where the barriers between the known and unknown are breached with ease.

The other observation from Janet Murray which resonates with Natalie's story is her comment upon the way in which one art form takes the techniques of another and develops them. Murray cites the example of how the cinema refined Charles Dickens' practice of inserting cross cuts between intersecting stories, or Emily Brontë's complex use of flashback (Murray 1997: 29). One of the most interesting characteristics of Natalie's work is its filmic qualities. The story opens, for example, with an 'establishing shot' depicting castles, apples, trees, grass, flowers. Most effective of all, however, is the section in the second paragraph – enhanced by the attempt at ellipsis – where the 'camera' zooms in on the giant's face and pulls away again. The spelling and punctuation are reproduced as in the original:

> The smile on the giants face disapered. He came running over. . . .

Natalie's use of dialogue and commentary is sophisticated. Only when the giant's words deflate the tension does the narrator reveal just how scared she was:

> 'Do you want to join us'. PHEW! I thought he was going to eat me!

There is an economy of touch here – a powerful use of montage almost – that a film editor might envy.

Mark's 'story' hardly bears comparison; but he too deserves the teacher's due – that readerly respect and professional concern which Neil Corcoran has memorably characterized as 'alert and challenged acts of attention' (2009: 165). Where the focus of attention regarding Natalie's work might lie with her use of composition, a pressing concern in relation to Mark's writing is the need to explore secretarial issues, starting at the first, grapho phonemic, level of the writing code. What can we build on? Mark can form his letters correctly; and although the consistent, laborious use of print suggests an insecure grasp of fine motor skills, there is evidence – in the way that he forms the letters of *sed* or the *ald* of *feald* – that he is beginning to attempt a cursive handwriting style. Applying the morphological 'spectacle', we might feel concerned that the morpheme *s* is missing from the word *friend* and that the suffix *ed* has not been added to *walk* to indicate the past tense. Moving to the lexical level, we might note that Mark has spelled *friend, football* and *park* correctly (the opening line was copied from the board – and interestingly, unlike Natalie, Mark reproduced each word accurately). His misspelling of a high frequency word like *sed* is at least logical and consistent; and the misspelling of *feald* is, again, logical if one thinks of a word like *weald*.

What can be said about this piece from a compositional perspective, applying the sixth, textual, 'spectacle'? The first point to make is that, let down by his lack of fine motor skills, Mark did not have time to do more than provide the opening paragraph of his story (note the words 'we saw a' crossed out at the bottom of the piece) before he was obliged to stop. How differently from Natalie he responds to the invitation of the prompt line: the remarkable sight which greets the persona in his story is nothing more unusual than his friend, Dan. Rather than being transported to a fantasy world of castles and giants bearing magical watches, the two boys exchange terse greetings and play football in the familiar world of the park. The 'simple, literal, affirmative' sentences deployed by Mark here are characteristic, according to Wilkinson et al. of children's early writing (1980: 3) – and again, Vygotsky's point about the mismatch between chronological age and intellectual development is starkly brought to mind. Mark's potential as a writer lies in the last, uncompleted and discarded phrase of his curtailed story. If, in Murray's phrase, our task as teachers is to help him 'to be aware of . . . alternative possible selves, of alternative possible worlds', this is where our work with him must start.

The following chart is a useful means of recording information about the two young writers (Natalie first):

Table 1.2

Using assessment to inform work with Natalie's Zone of Proximal Development

Level of the Writing Code	Can do	Ready to attempt with help
Grapho-phonemic	Letters clearly formed, some attempt at a cursive handwriting style.	Move away from printing to development of a fully cursive handwriting style; developments of alternatives to capitalization (and exclamation marks) to create dramatic effects in writing.
Morphological	Secure knowledge of how suffixes can indicate tense and pluralisation.	Pluralisation of words ending in 'f'; securing of spelling of root word 'appear'; use of apostrophe for possession.
Lexical	Secure knowledge of (and ability to spell accurately) words associated with fairy stories.	More imaginative use of adjectives and adverbs (alternatives to 'big', 'huge', 'lovely').
Syntactic	Generally secure use of simple sentences; some evidence of subordinate clauses and post modification; some understanding of conventions regarding the writing of dialogue; use of ellipsis to indicate suspense; has some understanding of paragraphing.	Differences between commas and full stops; complex sentences including pre as well as post modification; further use of ellipsis and other techniques for developing atmosphere in fictional writing; further engagement with the writing of dialogue; more imaginative and sophisticated use of paragraphing to create effect.

(Continued)

Table 1.2 Cont'd

Textual	Understands the basic conventions of narrative, including structure, chronology, perspective and voice; some awareness of the genre conventions regarding fairy stories.	Editorial skills, in order to distinguish between promising and unpromising elements of her writing; experiments with chronology, voice and structure; alternatives to clichéd story endings.
Contextual	Strong visual sense, with some ability to draw effectively upon cinematic techniques.	Techniques of montage, flash-back, cutting; wider engagement with the fairy tale genre, including texts from different cultures and stories which subvert the conventions of the genre.

Using assessment to inform work with Mark's Zone of Proximal Development

Level of the Writing Code	Can do	Ready to attempt with help
Grapho-phonemic	Print letters accurately, including capital letters for names; some attempt at cursive handwriting.	Further development of cursive handwriting style, beginning with the 'se' letter combination which he has already started to secure.
Morphological	Spell the word 'football' accurately; understand the spelling of 'friend' and apply a rule to the (mis)spelling of 'feald'.	Engagement with other compound nouns and, thence, with the concept of prefixes, suffixes and root words; work on phonic strategies with particular relation to blends, digraphs and letter string patterns.
Lexical	Spell words which feature prominently in his life: 'friend', 'park', 'football'.	Enrichment of vocabulary through engagement with language in purposeful contexts.
Syntactic	Write simple sentences consisting mainly of literal statements; understand the role of simple connectives like 'and'; show some awareness of the conventions regarding speech marks.	Consolidation of understanding about the structure of a simple sentence and the function of the full stop; introduction of different connectives to prepare for introductory work on clauses; consolidation of rules regarding the use of speech marks.
Textual	Show some understanding of the conventions of narrative including the use of dialogue, the introduction of characters and the telling of a story in chronological sequences.	Engagement with other writers' narratives (but also, crucially, other genre forms) which celebrate football and friendship.
Contextual	Understands that writing can record (and celebrate) important events and relationships.	Engagement with a range of genres beyond narrative fiction; understanding that male role models place value upon the power of the written and spoken word in both its fictional and non-fictional forms.

Reflection Activity 1.3

Choose two pieces of work produced in your classroom by students of widely differing abilities. Analyse the work against the levels of the writing code as we have done above with the assignments written by Mark and Natalie. How can national and school based data help to inform your analysis of their current achievement and their learning needs? What other information would you require to give you a more rounded picture? Consider the implications for your short, medium and long term planning.

It is important to emphasize that what is provided here is nothing more than a snapshot of Mark and Natalie's potential development as writers – a snapshot, moreover, that was produced in circumstances which, involving as they did a decontextualized exercise written under timed pressure – were far from ideal. To establish a clearer and more accurate picture, we would not only need to consult the statistical information described earlier in the chapter, but also to compile for both students an assessment portfolio across all four modalities of English. It is important to be a little circumspect with a statement like this, however. One of the major misconceptions regarding differentiation – and this point is revisited particularly in Chapter 5 – is that it involves designing a detailed educational plan for each individual in the class – and this is why hard pressed teachers can be tempted into either dismissing differentiation as an impossibly idealistic aspiration or going for the easy option of differentiation by outcome.

Time to recall again the pragmatic counsel of Jonothan Neelands cited at the start of the chapter. A compromise which is both logistically feasible and more likely to help teachers retain their sanity is to look for *patterns* of need, ability and interest within the community of the classroom. For an example, let us take a closer look at the learning agenda we established for Mark and Natalie under the *textual* level of the writing code. Mark would benefit from exploring a range of narratives and other genre forms; Natalie would benefit from refining her editorial skills, experimenting with chronology, voice and structure and from considering alternatives to clichéd story endings. It is highly unlikely that they will be the only members of the class who need to work in these areas. One practical way forward within the confines of the classroom therefore might be to *differentiate our work by task:* everyone is involved in, say, a writing activity but the nature of that activity differs depending upon the particular needs of the individuals working within a specific student grouping. We might divide our class into four task groups, as outlined in Table 1.3 below:

Table 1.3

Group 1	Group 2	Group 3	Group 4
Editorial skills	*Chronology and Structure*	*Voice*	*Story endings*
Writing conference: students respond to each other's timed stories. The reader offers two items of praise and suggests one point for further consideration. The writer responds to this advice and, if appropriate, reworks the story accordingly.	Students redraft their stories without using the conventional narrative sequence of beginning, middle and end. They are encouraged to use flashbacks and to insert clues which give the readers hints about the conclusion.	Students rewrite their stories from an alternative point of view. For example, Natalie might rewrite *A different world* from the perspective of the giant. Students are asked to think about how the change of perspective influences our reading of the story.	Students compare the endings to their various stories: do they fall into patterns? Students compare their story endings with those found in fairy stories – for example: *and they all lived happily ever after.* Students explore a number of stories which have unexpected endings and redraft their own, so that they have a 'twist'.

Accessing powerful curriculum: alternatives to differentiation by outcome

Commentating upon what they perceive to be the key issues informing differentiation, Tomlinson and McTighe suggest that:

> two of the greatest contemporary challenges for educators [are] crafting powerful curriculum . . . and ensuring academic success for the full spectrum of learners . . . (2006: 2)

One could argue that the example of differentiation by task outlined in Table 1.3 above meets the criterion regarding the 'crafting' of 'powerful curriculum'. The activities described are not meant simply to keep students busy; they are devised to meet a perceived learning need. Logistically, too, there are advantages to be gained from differentiating by task: that potentially daunting collection of 30 individuals has been reorganized into four more manageable groups of learners. Issues still remain, however. Tomlinson and McTighe's point about 'the full spectrum of learners' is problematic. Each of the tasks suggested above assumes a certain facility with the skills of writing (and reading). This might be fine for Natalie but not – judging on the basis of the story he produced – for Mark. It would be tempting to respond by withdrawing him and any other students who shared his difficulties from the main body of the lesson so that they could receive remedial support. To adopt such a course, however, would be to imply that students cannot access 'powerful curriculum' until they have mastered basic skills. Nothing could be more antithetical to the principle of differentiation. If we believe that the classroom is a community of learners and that each student in our care matters to us, then we have a moral duty to ensure that Mark is granted the same curriculum entitlement as Natalie.

One person who can help here is Howard Gardner. Gardner's theory that intelligence can be expressed in eight different ways – ranging from the *linguistic* to the *intrapersonal* – is not without criticism (e.g. White 2000; see also Chapter 3); however, it has made a welcome contribution to our thinking about differentiation. As Kornhaber puts it:

> the theory validates educators' everyday experience: students think and learn in many different ways. It also provides educators with a conceptual framework for organizing and reflecting on curriculum assessment and pedagogical practices. In turn, this reflection has led many educators to develop new approaches that might better meet the needs of the range of learners in their classrooms. (2001: 276)

Gardner argues that intelligence is the capacity to solve problems in one or more cultural settings (Gardner and Hatch 1989). The word *more* is significant here. Is it essential that Mark access the curriculum opportunities implicit in the activities described in Table 1.3 above *only* through the media of writing and reading? The answer depends upon the nature of the learning outcome which those activities are meant to promote. Take as an example from Table 1.3 *Group Two: Chronology and Structure*. The intended learning outcome could be recast as the following question:

> How can we make our written stories more interesting by experimenting with the 'beginning, middle and end' convention?

For Mark, the adjective modifying the noun *stories* will cause problems. If the desired learning outcome is to be evidenced by a piece of accomplished writing, then his chances of success – given his restricted fine motor skills, his insecure grasp of the conventions of narrative prose and his limited written vocabulary – will be severely curtailed, just as they were in the original exercise. Suppose, however, that the adjective was removed from the *learning outcome* question? Mark is then allowed not only to engage with the constructionist possibilities implicit in the present participle *experimenting;* he is also granted access to the 'big idea' about narrative structure which lies at the core of the question.

A classroom desk might not be the appropriate 'cultural setting' for Mark to begin his attempt to solve the problem posed by the learning outcome question. Judging from the way that his brief story moves so quickly onto the subject of football, it might be that he feels more secure working with what Gardner calls *Bodily-Kinaesthetic* intelligence and that he would welcome the opportunity to engage with the question in a very different 'cultural setting' – such as a Drama space, perhaps. You might wish to bear this point in mind again when you encounter the references to Bernstein in Chapter 3 or to Barker and Gibson in Chapter 4. Some of the *Group Two* pupils might therefore be given an alternative brief: to interrogate and to interact physically with Mark's story as if it were a play script. Here we move into a consideration of *differentiation by support.* Fundamental to this strategy is Jerome Bruner's concept of *scaffolding* (Wood et al. 1976): the process by which a teacher – or, significantly, a peer – encourages a move towards independent learning by first creating a framework of support around a student and then gradually withdrawing it as the learner moves towards *internalization* (Applebee and Langer 1983) and *self actualization* (Maslow 1954). In the example explored here, we could say that the process of scaffolding actually began when the teacher removed the adjective *written* from the learning outcome question. Finding the right questions to ask is crucial to the whole enterprise of differentiation: they either allow students access to 'powerful curriculum' or they shut them out. Lange (2002) suggests that scaffolding is effected by the use of such strategies as *modelling, explaining, inviting participation* or *clarifying understanding.* The example below attempts to show how we might apply some of these strategies to support Mark's access to Tomlinson and McTighe's 'powerful curriculum'.

Recalling Gardner's point about different cultural settings and Bruner's focus upon 'subjunctivizing reality', our first move might be to think of Mark's story not as an indifferent, poorly conceived fragment of time-pressured writing but as a drama script. This not only has the benefit of introducing him to a wider range of genre (see his *ready to achieve with help* entry for the *contextual* level of the writing code above); it also shifts the focus from what is deficient about the piece to what its potential might be as a way into learning. Viewed in this way, the story can be considered as a sequence of four prompts around each of which a scaffold of support can be erected.

Table 1.4

Prompt	Scaffolding Strategies (Lange: 2002)	Enabling Question(s)	Activities
When I looked over the wall, I could hardly believe my eyes!	Modelling Explaining Inviting participation	Can we think of times in our lives when we have been surprised? How do people express surprise through their body, the words they say and the way they say those words?	Group sharing of stories Freeze frames Spontaneous improvisation
I saw one of my friends – his name was Dan.	Explaining Inviting participation Clarifying understanding	Why might the boy in the story have been so surprised to see his friend Dan? What do we make of the fact that the narrator does not demonstrate any emotion when he introduces Dan into the story – even though he was so surprised to see him?	Group explores a number of possible explanations, drawing upon their own experiences of friendship if they feel comfortable with doing so. Spontaneous and/or prepared improvisations creating a 'back story' to contextualise the encounter between the narrator and Dan.
He walked over to me and he said: 'Hello'; so I said the same.	Inviting participation Clarifying understanding	What registers do we use to greet different people? What does the way in which the narrator and Dan greet each other tell us about their relationship? How else might they have greeted each other? Do the back stories we created for the narrator and Dan accord with the way they greet each other here, or do we need to modify those stories in the light of this information?	Group discussion about the concept of 'register' and about the ways in which the back stories might help to illuminate the relationship between the narrator and Dan. Pairs act out the greeting between the narrator and Dan, 'freezing' the action at the point which they feel to be most significant in providing clues about the relationship between the two boys.
We went to the park and played football on the field.	Explaining Inviting participation Clarifying understanding	What do we mean when we use a phrase like *Actions speak louder than words?* Are there times in our lives when we find it easier to show what we feel for another person by doing something with them rather than by talking?	Group sharing of stories in response to the questions leads into a consideration of 'ritual', 'subtext' and 'narrative closure'.

(Continued)

Table 1.4 Cont'd

Prompt	Strategies (Lange: 2002)	Enabling Questions	Activities
		Can we think of occasions when we do this as a family, or community or society? What do we feel about the ending to this story? How does it accord with the back stories we created earlier? What other endings might the author have devised? Do stories ever really 'end'?	Students consider the differences between 'naturalism' and 'ritual'. Using appropriate theatrical conventions, they devise and present either a naturalistic or ritualised dramatic representation to mark the end of Mark's story.

If strategies for differentiation by support like the ones described above are implemented successfully, they can work powerfully to effect those transformations which are the goal of all educational endeavour. So here: a piece of text which seemed to do no more than advertise Mark's deficiencies as a writer is transformed into a potent means of engagement with 'powerful curriculum'. To borrow the poet WB Yeats' famous metaphors about learning, Mark himself is transformed from a passive 'bucket' waiting to be filled with knowledge by the teacher into a 'fire' capable of igniting the spark of intellectual curiosity in himself and those around him (it is no accident that Lange's scaffolding strategies are composed of active verbs; and you should bear this point carefully in mind when we explore taxonomies of learning in more detail in Chapters 4 and 5). This experience in itself will help him start to reclaim that 'joy of discovery' which Graves described. His sense of confidence will be immeasurably enhanced if the teacher – and English practitioners committed to a 'personal growth' agenda which places at the heart of the curriculum the idea of the child as active meaning-maker (Dixon 1967) are particularly well-placed to do this – affords their pupils' work those 'alert and challenged acts of attention' described by Corcoran earlier in the chapter. I suspect that, when he wrote his story under such difficult circumstances, Mark was completely unaware of the interesting possibilities afforded by the first sentence of his response to the prompt *When I looked over the wall I could hardly believe my eyes.* What matters is that the teacher, studying the piece of writing through the lenses which Vygotsky has given us, saw the learning potential implicit in Mark's seemingly unpromising response, treated it with the seriousness and respect one might afford a canonical writer, and exploited it as a way into powerful learning. Crucially here, the teacher does not fall into the trap of palming Mark off with some impoverished version of the learning outcome. The activities described above could be used to investigate narrative structure at a most sophisticated level. One could, for example, explore the use of back story as a way into Gérard Genette's concept of *analepsis* (1972) or consider the narrator's surprise at seeing his friend Dan as an example of Roland Barthes' *hermeneutic code* in action (1970), or tease out in dramatic terms the complex semiology of the game of football which closes Mark story (Eco 1998).

There is a danger that the kinds of differentiation described in Table 1.4 above – four separate groups working on four distinct sets of activities – serve only to confirm those concerns about segregation and lack of access voiced by Brian Simon at the start of the chapter. Are we creating a situation where Mark and Natalie, though physically present in the same room, never actually meet in terms of learning and shared experience? If that is the case, why not say, bleakly, that they have nothing at all to gain either socially or intellectually from interacting with each other? After all, we noted earlier how their written work suggests that their life chances have already begun to harden along lines of class and privilege – why not simply help that process along by putting them in separate rooms? One way round this problem could be to differentiate by *menu, text* and *pace*. If we consider the activities suggested in Table 1.4 for *Group Two*, it must be clear that they present fruitful opportunities for Natalie, just as much as for Mark, to address the learning goals identified at the *textual* level of the writing code.

Another way of configuring our central strategy of differentiating by *support*, therefore – one which preserves the integrity of the class as a whole community of learners and upholds the principles of equal access and of shared experience – might be to set up an initial core activity which everyone in the class undertakes *before* selecting, like a course from a *menu* (hence the metaphor) to work in one of the four groupings described in Table 1.4. Staying with our same learning outcome question and imagining this time that both Mark and Natalie are exploring the *Chronology and Structure* strand of activities, we might construct a differentiated learning pathway which leads out from (and, crucially, *back to*) the core activity.

Differentiation of this kind really requires the teacher to exchange Petty's metaphor of 'the knife' for that of 'the spectacles' so that we can 'look at the *whole* from *different points of view*' as he put it earlier. To prepare ourselves thoroughly, we might not only engage with Gardner's theory of multiple intelligences, but also explore the writings of those psychologists who, building upon the pioneering work of Carl Jung, have investigated patterns of learning style and personality trait – for example, Kolb's *Learning Style Inventory* (1975) (for more on Kolb, see Chapter 3). If that seems too costly in terms of time for the hard-pressed teacher, we can at the very least attempt an holistic understanding of our students by getting to know them in extra curricular contexts, talking to others who teach them or to family members, observing in lessons the ways in which they seem to learn effectively and, perhaps most important, encouraging them to reflect upon and gain some understanding of their own preferred learning styles (see also the detailed analysis of Melanie's power point presentation in Chapter 3).

Getting to know 'the child behind the text', as Andrews put it, takes a real investment of time and effort; and perhaps therefore the kind of differentiation described in this final section of the chapter is something which teachers will feel most comfortable using once they have established a strong working relationship with the individuals in their class. Nevertheless, it has teased out some significant final points. We have already considered *differentiation by menu;* but no less important here is the concept of *differentiation by pace.* Just as we said that Mark was morally entitled to 'powerful curriculum', so it is equally important to assert that principles of equality and entitlement do not mean that Natalie should not be challenged to give of her best (You might wish to bear this point in mind when you consider Laura's response to *The Lady of Shalott* in Chapter 3). In the activities cited below, Natalie accesses the same powerful learning outcome question but at a faster pace and at a conceptually higher level:

Table 1.5

Core activity Natalie/Mark	Teacher introduces *analepsis* and the *hermeneutic code* and illustrates them with examples from written narrative and/or film. Sharing the first two lines of Mark's story with the class, teacher suggests that Mark has set up a puzzle in the opening of his story (why is the narrator so astonished to see his friend?) The students are invited to speculate about possible solutions to that puzzle and then to write, dictate, record as an MP3 file or perform their version of the back story
Follow up activity Natalie's group	Students explore a range of extracts from fiction in which characterisation is particularly vivid. They are asked to consider the techniques used by the authors to achieve this effect and then to write a second version of the back story, this time from the point of view of Dan. In their writing, they should make explicit use of some of the authorial techniques explored in their reading.
Follow up activity Mark's group (See also *scaffolding* diagrams)	Guided by careful questioning from the teacher, students follow up their initial explorations of possible back story solutions to Mark's narrative puzzle through a sequence of drama exercises, improvisations and theatre forms. They look for moments of significance, consider the concept of narrative closure and think about the differences between ritualistic and naturalistic presentation.

(Continued)

Table 1.5 Cont'd

Core activity (Plenary) Natalie/Mark	The groups come back together to share their respective responses to the learning outcome question through a mutual exchange and analysis of story. Natalie's group read examples from their written work and explain how they used techniques of characterisation to give Dan a real voice in the story. Mark's group present their dramatised interpretations of possible story endings, explaining what they have learned about the concept of narrative closure. *All* students are invited to capture the learning. They might make notes in their exercise books, for example, or create 'word wall' posters and graphic organisers to place around the classroom for further reference. The teacher invites Natalie to reflect specifically upon what she has learned about narrative voice from her group's work and on what she has learned about narrative closure from Mark's group's work. Mark is invited to reflect upon what he has learned about significant narrative detail from his group's work on back story and narrative closure and on what he has learned about descriptive writing from Natalie's group's work on voice.

Where Mark's learning has an oral focus and is scaffolded by skilful questioning within the security of teacher (and peer) supported discussion and practical work, Natalie is invited to address the learning outcome question in a different 'cultural setting'. Differentiating through *resource, interest* and *text,* her teacher has asked her to engage with the written rather than the spoken word by exploring a range of style models provided by powerful practitioners of narrative fiction. The same attention to pace might be afforded to Natalie's access to metalanguage: where Mark is encouraged to engage with and secure words like *narrator* or *register,* Natalie might be requested to reflect explicitly upon Barthes' reading codes or Genette's organizational devices for the shaping of narrative.

We began this chapter by imagining an English teacher looking into 30 expectant, 11-year-old faces at the start of their secondary school careers and thinking how set their life chances already seemed at such a young age. If education is really to effect transformation, than differentiation – or *personalized learning* or whatever currently fashionable guise it takes – must, for ethical as well as pedagogical reasons – inform everything we do in the classroom. Chapters 3 and 4 will revisit these crucially important points.

Reflection Activity 1.4

Consider again the zone of proximal development for the two writers whose work you analysed in Reflection Activity 1.3. Devise a sequence of lessons which draws upon the following differentiation strategies: **task, pace, interest** and **support**. Your lesson plans must include purposeful opportunities for the two pupils to work together.

Emotional Intelligence

2

Key Questions

The following key questions underpin the chapter:

1. What do we mean by emotional intelligence and why should it matter to English teachers?

2. What pressures does the task of responding to students' writing in our role as trusted adult place upon the teacher?

3. Can we reconcile different teaching and learning agendas in the classroom?

4. How might an engagement with literature help us to achieve this reconciliation?

Emotional Intelligence: what is it and why should it matter to English teachers?

The chapter on differentiation began by focussing upon the particular learning needs of two individual students. This chapter has a similar starting point; but it explores the writing of a student called Asif who, although he shares some of the same concerns, is in others very different from either Mark or Natalie. Like Mark and Natalie, Asif is new to his school, though not for the same reasons: born in Malaysia 15 years ago, he has recently moved with his family to England. Although working in an unfamiliar second language, Asif is a quick learner and has been entered for his English General Certificate in Secondary Education (GCSE). Asked to produce a piece of coursework for the 'Original Writing' component of the syllabus, he hands his teacher an account of the sudden, tragic death of his younger brother.

Are there any English teachers who have not, in the course of their careers, known at least one moment like this? A student – Asif in this chapter, Melanie in Chapter 3 – shares a deeply personal, often harrowing experience and turns to their teacher, as trusted adult, for a response.

This is why the issues associated with the concept of 'emotional intelligence' speak particularly powerfully to us. The term – together with its close neighbour, 'emotional literacy' (Steiner and Perry 1997) – came to prominence in the last decade of the twentieth century, largely through the work of Salovey and Mayer (1993, 1997) and, perhaps most popularly, Daniel Goleman. Goleman defines emotional intelligence in terms of the following abilities:

> being able to motivate oneself and persist in the face of frustrations; to control impulse and delay gratification; to regulate one's moods and keep distress from swamping the ability to think; to empathize and to hope. (Goleman 1996: 34)

Like Howard Gardner's theory of multiple intelligences on which it builds, Goleman's concept of emotional intelligence is not without its critics (e.g. Eysenck 2000, Landy 2005, Locke 2005; see also Chapter 3); however, these criticisms do not mean that Goleman has nothing of importance to say to English teachers. At the very least, he obliges us to remember that our students are not some anonymous, amorphous mass but – like the girls we will meet in Chapter 5 – sentient individuals with their own personalities, temperaments, moods and dispositions. As Tomlinson and McTighe put it:

> A teacher who arrives in the classroom . . . is likely to stand before students of advanced ability and students who come trailing disabilities, students from poverty and students from plenty, students who dream bold dreams and students who do not believe dreams are worth their time, students who speak the language of power and students to whom that language is unfamiliar, students who learn by listening and those who learn through application, students who are compliant and those who challenge authority on every hand, students who trust and those who are damaged and devoid of trust. To pretend those differences do not matter in the teaching/learning process is to live an illusion.

Taking responsibility for the welfare of such a diverse range of human beings places significant obligations upon the teacher. Tomlinson and McTighe continue:

> Toward that end, they [our students] come to the classroom first looking for things like affirmation, affiliation, accomplishment, and autonomy . . . They are looking for adults who accept them, value them, guide them, and represent for them what it means to be a competent and caring adult. (2006: 16)

Reflection Activity 2.1

Consider a class of students that you teach. What do you really know about them as individuals? The way they like to learn? Their interests? Their home backgrounds? Their hopes and fears? How might you get to know them better, both within and outside the classroom? Who – within and beyond the school context – might help you to do this?

This alone is enough to give the teacher of English pause for thought. If Goleman does no more than encourage us to mindful classroom practice in the selection and dissemination of our chosen material – so that we hesitate before deciding, for example, to explore a poem like Seamus Heaney's *Mid-Term Break* with a student who has suffered a bereavement, or consider carefully the implications of teaching Shakespeare's *Othello* to a student for whom issues of prejudice and bigotry are painfully raw – then we will have gained something important from an engagement with the concept of 'emotional intelligence', no matter how problematic critics may find it.

A second reason, however, why it is important for English teachers particularly to consider carefully what Goleman says (and to accept the challenge proffered by Tomlinson and McTighe in the quotation cited above) is that the principles of emotional intelligence accord so clearly with some of the most established and cherished tenets of English pedagogy.

It is significant that when, in the late 80s of the past century, Brian Cox was invited to draw up a National Curriculum for English in England and Wales which would present an approach broad enough to 'unite the profession', the model he placed first on his list was the following:

> A 'personal growth' view focuses on the child: it emphasises the relationship between language and learning in the individual child, and the role of literature in developing children's imaginative and aesthetic lives. (Cox 1991: 21)

The beliefs expressed here by Cox can be traced back at least as far as the late nineteenth century when the poet (and school inspector) Matthew Arnold declared that literature is 'the greatest power available in education' and that poetry in particular 'undoubtedly tends to form the soul and character' (in Mathieson 1975: 44). These twin commitments to what Peter Abbs memorably describes as 'the unfolding and elaboration of self through activity, intellectual enquiry and creative play' on the one hand and to 'significant literature as a formative pressure on existence' on the other (Abbs 1982: 10 and 13) run like vivid, intertwining threads through the fabric of twentieth-century English teaching. As the arguments about what should constitute the content and concerns of 'subject English' have grown ever more diverse – to the extent that the teacher of English is in danger of becoming, as Abbs puts it, 'like a man carrying a bag of tools but with only other people's jobs to do' – (1982: 10) so the idea of the child as an imaginative, creative, *emotional* receiver and maker of meanings (Dixon 1967) has increasingly come to represent an organizing principle which can bring coherence and even claims of uniqueness to the subject. Writing (prophetically) almost 30 years ago about the dangers inherent in 'the drone of a new technicism', Abbs concluded:

> What had been overlooked in the pathological obsession for communications was the elusive underground of the psyche, those preconceptual sources of latent formulation locked in the emergent impulses of the body and the unconscious. Only by maintaining contact with these deeper pre-verbal energies can language itself remain resonant, charged, rich, strange, compelling and worthwhile. (1982: 21)

Those arguments still speak persuasively to English teachers who, when asked to declare their preferences among Cox's five models of English – *personal growth, cross-curricular, adult needs, cultural heritage* and *cultural analysis* – consistently place *personal growth* high on the list (Goodwyn 1992, Marshall

2000, Hardman 2001, Smagorinsky 2002). Goleman would not be surprised. Arguing that 'some of us are naturally more attuned to the emotional mind's special symbolic modes: metaphor and simile', he suggests that the discourses of literature are particularly appropriate for 'the language of the heart' (1996: 54) and that teachers who work with story, fable and ritual – as English practitioners committed to a *personal growth* agenda do – can be its most effective champions:

> The logic of the emotional mind is associative; it takes elements that symbolize a reality, or trigger a memory of it, to be the same as that reality. That is why similes, metaphors and images speak directly to the emotional mind, as do the arts – novels, film, poetry, song, theater, opera. Great spiritual teachers, like Buddha and Jesus, have touched their disciples' hearts by speaking in the language of emotion, teaching in parables, fables, and stories. (1996: 294)

In its most extreme form, the *personal growth* model of English can construct the child as some kind of Blakean innocent who, like Rousseau's Emile, must be defended against the perceived depredations of society at all cost. Here, for example, is George Sampson, writing in the aftermath of the Great War and from his experience of teaching in the elementary schools of London's East End:

> I am prepared to maintain, and indeed, do maintain, without reservation and perhapses, that it is the purpose of education, not to prepare children for their occupations, but to prepare children against their occupations. (1925: 11)

Here too Goleman seems prepared to follow. There is something almost apocalyptic about his vision for the future. Arguing that 'a new kind of toxicity' is 'sweeping into and poisoning the very experience of childhood' (1996: 233) he warns that the 'millennial years are ushering in an Age of Melancholy, just as the twentieth century became an Age of Anxiety' (1996: 240).

It is not only the concerns associated with emotional intelligence which align so closely with core beliefs espoused by English teachers. Its remedial procedures, too, are those which we would recognize as fundamental to our classroom practice. This is hardly surprising, given that one of our key endeavours – the teaching of effective communication with oneself and with others – is regarded as the essence of emotional intelligence. Thus, Goleman, Salovey and Meyer, and Steiner all emphasize the importance of being able to *read* one's own emotions and those of others. Indeed, Goleman identifies the condition of *dyssemia* – the inability to interpret social and emotional signs – as a major contributor to students' failure to flourish at school. Similarly, Mortiboys, (2005) taking his cue from clinical psychologist Carl Rogers' assertion that 'the creation of an atmosphere of acceptance, understanding and respect' should be 'the basis for the learning which is called education' (Rogers 1951: 384) stresses the need for teachers to cultivate strategies, not only for speaking with sensitivity in the classroom, but perhaps even more importantly, for listening with patience, tact and understanding. Asher's (1987) programme of 'friendship coaching' – designed to teach socially insecure children the skills they need to integrate into the school community – focuses upon turn-taking, negotiation, positive use of body-language and sensitive listening. This is the kind of good practice to which all English teachers committed to effective oracy aspire.

Complaining about what he perceives to be a 'lack of recognition of the importance of emotional intelligence for teachers ... in teacher training courses at all levels', Mortiboys asserts:

> There is no part of the curriculum in which the trainee teacher is asked, 'Who are you and how do you relate to other people?' (2005: 3)

English teachers committed to a *personal growth* curriculum model might dispute this. When we hear advocates of emotional intelligence (e.g. Terr 1990) emphasize the importance of articulating and thus gaining some purchase on our emotions or experiences by shaping them into spoken, written or dramatic narrative, we might recall the words of John Dixon, English teacher and champion of the *personal growth* model, who argued that it is our business to help students create their 'own representational world' through language, because:

> In ordering and composing situations that in some way symbolise life as we know it, we bring order and composure to our inner selves. (1967: 20)

And where, outside the literature classroom or the Drama studio, is there a more effective pedagogical space for young people to be afforded what Bernstein in Chapter 3 will describe as the 'acoustic' of school so that they might explore, in a safely fictional context, Mortiboys' vital questions about identity and relationships?

Reflection Activity 2.2

Where do you stand regarding the debate about emotional intelligence? Is it just a fashionable fad, or does it lie at the core of what you believe English teaching is all about? What brought you into the classroom? Are you able to teach in a way which fulfils you as an autonomous, creative professional, or do you feel that you are having to work to somebody else's agenda? Which of the Cox models of English speak to you most powerfully?

Case Study: Asif writes about the death of his brother

For this next section of the chapter, I feel impelled to write in the personal voice; for I am the teacher to whom a 15-year-old boy called Asif brought his piece of personal writing to read. On receiving it, I need to be mindful of Goleman's observation that childhood provides 'a crucial window of opportunity for shaping lifelong emotional propensities' and that 'the frontal lobes [of the brain] – seat of emotional self-control, understanding and artful response – continue to develop into late adolescence' (1996: 226). In other words, it is important to interpret his action as an appeal for the 'affirmation' and 'affiliation' which Tomlinson and McTighe describe and as a consequence of that I as his teacher might see my role as deploying those skills of emotional intelligence described by Mortiboys so that I can help him articulate, understand and thus gain a measure of control over the terrible, life-changing event he has described in his story.

This is how the piece opens. The spelling and punctuation is as it was in the original.

Fifteen September, six fourty seven o'clock. I wake up from the sleep. It is still dark. I look around me. My brother is still not awake from the sleep. I jump from the bed and go down to the dining room.

On my way to the dining room, I heard the phone ringing. I quickly run down and answer the phone.

'Hello, who's talking?'

'It's me, grand ma!'

I know she wants to have a chat with my mum so i quickly wake her up. Both of them keep talking until the clock show seven.

The weather outside is windy. I look at my mum. A second later after she put down the phone, she asked me to wake everyone up. She also asked me to settle my disabled brother. I wake everyone up and go back downstairs.

Case Study—Cont'd

> As I arrived, i go sit next to my brother and turn him around. i could not believe what is happening. Blood has come out through his nose and mouth and his body is very cold. I quickly shout out loud calling my mum and dad to go down stairs.

As with the stories by Mark and Natalie reproduced in the chapter on differentiation, and the powerful oral presentation from Melanie which follows this chapter, the teacher's work with Asif begins by applying Vygotsky's concept of the zone of proximal development to the writing he has offered here. It is important to afford that writing the same degree of care and attention that was given to the work of the two younger students in Chapter 1; but this time there is a subtle difference in the way I approach the text – I bring to it Geoff Petty's metaphor, not of the forensic *knife*, but of the holistic *spectacles*. Where Mark and Natalie's work was written under timed conditions on a decontextualized topic and in a genre imposed by the teacher, Asif has exercised control over both the subject matter and the medium of expression for his writing. Moreover, he has used the opportunity afforded by the GCSE syllabus to do exactly what John Dixon or Daniel Goleman would wish the emotionally intelligent student to do: fashion through language a sensitive, heartfelt, articulate, informed and, ultimately, ordered response to the kind of horrific rite of passage which nobody would wish any young person to undergo.

The story concludes with the internment of Asif's brother back home in Malaya, to the accompaniment of age-old, almost timeless, burial rituals:

> We arrived in Malaysia. My grandsparents fetched us. The time was about halfpast four in the evening. It took about up to seven o'clock to get the body's out. Then we went to our villages. . . . That night we did a prayer for him and at nine thrity we interred him. before that i did touch him for the last time ever in my life.

Only when the obsequies have been observed and the story draws to its close, does Asif allow his emotions to show:

> That was the night that i will not forget all my life. When ever i'm reminded of him, i always cried by myself. I looked at the past when I was about eight years old when i tell him a funny story, sing for him and when ever i feel so sad, i always talk to him and tell him my feeling to him.

Reflection Activity 2.3

How would you respond if a student were to hand you a piece of writing as personal as this in response to an examination assessment? What if the student were to tell you that, as someone writing in an unfamiliar second language, he felt uncertain about whether or not he had used his past and present tense constructions correctly?

As an English teacher committed to a *personal growth* agenda and to the application of principles of emotional intelligence in the classroom, the context and subject matter of Asif's writing invest it with a moral and emotional authority which makes the wielding of Petty's assessment *knife* well-nigh impossible. I could in theory, as with Mark and Natalie's stories, analyse this piece against all seven levels of Andrews' writing code. In the extract quoted above, for example, I could note the inconsistent use of the upper case for the personal pronoun *I*, the misplaced apostrophe, the misspelling of *forty*, *thirty* and *grandparents* or, most poignantly, the uncertainty about whether to use the present or the past tense. But do these small errors of spelling, punctuation and orthography detract from the sheer force of what is being articulated here? And how insensitive would one have to be to suggest to Asif that he needs to choose a consistent tense for writing about his dead brother?

When engaging with this story, my urge is to put down Petty's *knife* and forget about Andrews' levels of the writing code. I simply want to respond as a human being to the beauty and the force of another human being's narrative. I want to take from it the aesthetic, moral and emotional consolations that powerful literature can bestow. On each of those levels, Asif's story is immensely enriching. Aesthetically, it is a very skilfully crafted piece of writing. Take the opening paragraph as an example. Each of those staccato sentences is like a carefully choreographed camera shot. We come to consciousness with the narrator, our eyes locked perhaps upon a digital alarm clock which is spelling out the date and time in a red, eerie glow against the darkness. Then the camera, still looking through the narrator's eyes, pans across the room and comes to rest upon the huddled shape of the brother, motionless and (so we think at this stage) still sleeping. In the next shot, the stillness and silence are broken as the narrator jumps out of bed and heads downstairs. The binary contrasts established in the paragraph are highly effective: darkness against light, silence against noise, sleep (or something worse) against wakefulness, movement against stillness, time against eternity. Morally, too, the piece speaks powerfully to me. The burial sequence of the story links it with the great tradition of writings about death and ritual that reaches back to classical texts such as the *Antigone*. Like Sophocles' play, Asif's story raises issues about our moral obligations to the dead and about the consoling ceremonies we devise to help us to weave the social fabric and to cope with the tragedies of life. Finally, the restrained, factual, almost deadpan narrative style adopted by the author serves to heighten the emotional impact of the story – an effect which is underscored when, in that final paragraph, Asif at last lets his pain show and, in doing so, speaks as artists can for all people who have endured similar experiences.

In other words, an emotionally intelligent reading of Asif's story has to move beyond the realms of objective criticism and dispassionate evaluation. When he brings his story to me, all that I really want to do is to thank him for letting me read it – perhaps, at most, to ask if he wants to talk about the experiences which inspired it. The last thing I would wish to do is to give the piece an examination grade. And yet this is exactly what Asif wants (and why the issues raised by his story are so pertinent to the concerns of this chapter). Anxious to master English quickly, he has brought this narrative to the public space of the examination classroom to receive objective critical scrutiny. He wants to be taught how to use the apostrophe correctly, how to spell words like *grandparents* and, most difficult of all from his teacher's perspective, how to distinguish the past from the present tense. On first reading his narrative, it would be understandable for a teacher to assume that Asif shared our commitment to the *personal growth* model of English and that he was writing within that context. In fact, he is actually concerned with claiming what Cox describes as the *adult needs* entitlement:

> An 'adult needs' view focuses on communication outside the school: it emphasises the responsibility of English teachers to prepare children for the language demands of adult life, including the workplace, in a fast-changing world. Children need to learn how to deal with the day-to-day demands of spoken language and of print; they also need to be able to write clearly, appropriately and effectively.
> (Cox 1991: 21)

The pitfalls of *dyssemia* and how to avoid them

How has this misunderstanding occurred? Ironically, both student and teacher engaged in the encounter appear to be displaying the *dyssemia* which Goleman identifies as one of the most negative consequences of the failure to apply emotional intelligence. There are powerful lessons to learn here. The first requires a thorough reappraisal of the channels of communication established in the classroom. If we cannot get those working correctly, we cannot hope to teach with emotional intelligence. Someone who can help us is Peter Griffith. He applies Jakobson's (1960) seminal work on the representation of 'the component elements of a speech event' (presented in diagrammatic form below) to the specific context of the English classroom:

Context

Message

Addresser ———————————— Addressee

Contact

Code

Griffith comments:

> For a *message* to be successfully transmitted there has also to be *contact,* which is a channel of communication . . . *code,* a series of recognizable symbols . . . and *context,* a mutually shared perception of situation. (1987: 2)

Each element of Jakobson's communication model has a function:

Referential

Poetic

Emotive ———————————— Conative

Phatic

Metalingual

Griffith glosses this diagram as follows:

> What Jakobson means by this second set of terms is that, if in a given speech event the focus is on the addresser ('How sad I am!') then the function is primarily *emotive.* If the focus is on the addressee ('Read the following three chapters') its function, a *conative* one, is to control or influence her or him in some way. When contact predominates ('Can you hear me, mother?') the function is *phatic,* checking that communication is being established. With code, a *metalingual* function carries out a somewhat similar activity but in respect of the code ('Excuse me, can you speak English?'). In the case of context, the *referential* function is concerned

> with the environment in which the speech event is taking place ('The two elements are forming a compound in the test-tube'). And, in Jakobson's view, when the focus is on the message itself as a self-conscious artefact, this is when we truly get the *poetic* function of language. (1987: 3–4)

Griffith cautions that, inevitably, Jakobson's model cannot hope to accommodate all the complexities of human communication; but if I had just taken the trouble to apply this template – imperfect though it might be – to my reading of Asif's story, I might have gone some way towards overcoming my *dyssemia* by realizing that my engagement with his writing so far has been all about *my* response and *my* needs as – to use Griffith's terminology – the *addressee* of this text. If I am to achieve that sense of empathy which Mortiboys considers to be the hallmark of the emotionally intelligent teacher, I need to shift the focus of my attention to the specific learning needs of the *addresser*:

> A prerequisite for responding to feelings expressed by others is the ability to step outside of our 'frame of reference' and into that of the other person. (2005: 75)

Applying Griffith's template, I can start to get a sense of where my misunderstandings occurred. Take the following lines from the opening of Asif's story as just one example:

> I wake up from the sleep. It is still dark. I look around me. My brother is still not awake from the sleep.

If I read these lines from the perspective of Griffith's *code* level, I can now see that Asif and I were at cross purposes in our interpretation of what ostensibly might seem to be 'a series of recognizable symbols'. Impelled by the force of the narrative, I chose to interpret the definite article in front of the word *sleep* as an effective literary device rather than seeing it for what it probably is – a grammatical error common to writers who are learning to express themselves in English as an additional language. Bringing a particularly Western-orientated sense of intertextuality to the story, the words evoke for me echoes of Raymond Chandler's novel *The Big Sleep* – the phrase itself a euphemism for death – and therefore they invest the opening of Asif's story with a chilling, prophetic resonance which the author did not deliberately intend. Eager to perfect his written English, Asif, on the other hand, would have been disappointed – embarrassed, even- to learn that he had misused the definite article – and, the lesson once learned, he would have taken pains not to repeat that mistake.

Clearly, too, misunderstandings have occurred at the *context* level of Griffith's communications model. Asif and I do not appear to have 'a mutually shared perception of situation' with regards to his story. Thinking in terms of Griffith's second diagram, I – as a teacher committed to a *personal growth* agenda – have interpreted the narrative as predominantly an *emotive* text whose function was to provide Asif with – in the words of Goleman quoted earlier – 'a crucial window of opportunity for shaping lifelong emotional propensities'. Again, there are cultural issues to consider here. The consolations which I, coming from my particular pedagogic and ideological tradition, imagine are to be found in what Abbs called 'the unfolding and elaboration of self', are afforded to Asif, not through the act of writing about them as I had supposed, but through his strong religious faith – as his story itself so movingly demonstrates. He, on the contrary, is more concerned with what Griffith calls a *conative* interpretation of his writing. He issues a call to action on my part as his teacher: he wants me to wield Petty's assessment *knife* so that he can achieve success in his examinations and become a fluent and effective writer of English.

Reflection Activity 2.4

Consider a lesson that you have taught recently. Analyse its channels of communication in terms of Griffith's template. How certain are you that you and all your students were 'reading' the lesson in the same ways? Where is your evidence for your answer? Did you and your students experience **dyssemia** during the lesson? How do you know this? What steps could you take in future to make sure that students and teacher are 'reading' each other and the lesson situation in the same way?

Reconciling different *frames of reference*

Does the fact that I have tried here to enter Asif's 'frame of reference' – as the principles of emotional intelligence dictate – mean that I have therefore to abandon my own? Mortiboys argues that to do so is 'unhealthy and not emotionally intelligent':

> This can lead to more stress for you and poor relationships with others if you are withholding your feelings from them. In doing this, you are not showing respect for yourself.

Emphasizing the need for 'self regulation' (Goleman 1996, Orme 2001) when such classroom encounters occur, Mortiboys counsels the emotionally intelligent teacher to:

> manage the feelings so that you can choose how to behave, looking after the interests of *both you and your learners* . . . [my italics] (2005: 122)

Mortiboys draws upon the Transactional Analysis theory devised by the Canadian psychiatrist Eric Berne (1964) to help teachers achieve this sense of self regulation. He suggests that there are 'five personal styles' which a teacher can use in the classroom and that these are based on three broad categories of *Parent, Adult* and *Child*. In the following extract, Mortiboys offers examples of typical statements which teachers might make when they adopt one of these roles:

> **Controlling Parent** – directing, firm
> 'Get into groups'
> 'I am going to stop you here because we must get on to the next activity'
> **Nurturing Parent** – caring, reassuring
> 'Don't worry if you can't finish this'
> 'Do you need me to explain that again?'
> **Adult** – problem solving, logical
> 'That is an interesting question'
> 'How do you think we should approach this problem?'
> **Natural Child** – spontaneous, creative, fun-loving
> 'Let's have some fun with this exercise'
> 'I am really excited about what you have just said'
> **Adapted Child** – compliant, polite OR rebellious, sulking
> 'Is it OK to open the window?'
> 'I would be very grateful if you could fill in this form before you
>   leave' (2005: 21)

Mortiboys argues:

> Unconsciously, we may be 'flipped' into a response that is triggered by what others say. More productive exchanges, certainly those more suitable to learning, can come about if we bring these transactions into our consciousness and take some control over them. (2005: 92–3)

Reflection Activity 2.5

Next time you teach a lesson, apply Berne's principles of Transactional Analysis to the exchanges which take place. What roles do you and your students play? To what extent are those role selections autonomous, conscious choices? Do you find yourself being forced to play particular roles by your students? How can you work towards a classroom situation where the majority of the transactions (or even all of them!) can be categorized as **adult to adult?**

Thinking about my exchange with Asif from this perspective reminds me that it reveals *dyssemia* on the part of the *student* as well as the teacher. If I have failed to appreciate that he is motivated by an *adult needs* agenda, then he for his part does not seem to have appreciated how a teacher committed to a *personal growth* curriculum model might respond to such an intimate and deeply-felt piece of writing. And what 'response' am I being 'flipped' into? By offering the story as a *conative* text, Asif is inviting me to play the role of – in Mortiboys' words – teacher as *controlling parent*: someone who will read the story as an example of inaccurate writing which needs correcting through the teaching of spelling and grammar rules.

I invited a group of trainee English teachers to see if they felt able to assess the piece in the way that Asif requested. They were asked to select, as a starting point for their response, an extract from the writing which had particularly engaged them. Here are three examples:

Trainee 1

Extract selected for comment from Asif's story
He said the body is settled. The body will be put in the packing place in the same plane. Well; at least I know he is still with us.

Trainee's response
'The body is settled' is a very good line because it is short which means your point is very exact but it shows his body and spirit combined have found peace.

Your last line 'I know he is still with us' is the kind of line that could apply to anyone who has lost someone; he was not only with you on the plane but he is with you forever in your thoughts.

You have said 'the body <u>will</u> be …' but it would make more sense to say 'the body would be …' because it is the future conditional tense: 'would have been'.

Trainee 2

Extract selected for comment from Asif's story
My brother went to tell the neighbour to give us a 'ride', to the hospital. No luck, they've gone to work. My mum went to called an ambulance and she even tried to get another neighbour that live not far from here.

Trainee's response
There is a real sense of movement and urgency which is underplayed - 'ride', 'no luck' – and only serves to make your mother's quest for an ambulance and help more poignant. However, try to avoid starting your second sentence in the same way as the first: 'My brother' and 'My mum'.

Trainee 3

Extract selected for comment from Asif's story
Once i had a dream in the past that he will get better, can walk, talk, at least he called or said ours names.

Trainee's response
I particularly liked your use of a three part list to show how desperate you were to see your brother again.

This powerful emotion is also emphasised through your use of a complex sentence which allows you to explore your feelings in detail.

The sentence would be even more powerful if you wrote in one particular tense. At the moment you are writing in the past and the present tense.

The use of the present tense 'we can talk' is effective, so why don't you try rewriting the whole sentence in the present tense? For example: 'I often have a dream'.

These three responses are typical of the cohort as a whole. Like me, the trainees have found it very difficult not to respond to this piece in what Mortiboys would describe as the role of *nurturing parent*. They consistently address the writer as 'you' and they focus their comments upon the descriptions and experiences which resonate for them as fellow human beings:

> Your last line 'I know he is still with us' is the kind of line that could apply to anyone who has lost someone; he was not only with you on the plane but he is with you forever in your thoughts.

Trainee 2 seems unable to accept Asif's request for a *conative* reading. No attempt is made to engage with the tense confusions of *went to called* or *another neighbour that live* and a rather bland stylistic suggestion, unrelated to Asif's key concerns, is offered instead:

> try to avoid starting your second sentence in the same way as the first: 'My brother' and 'My mum'.

The other way the trainee teachers seem to try to cope with Asif's challenge is to concentrate, dispassionately, upon the story in terms of its rhetorical effects:

> There is a real sense of movement and urgency which is underplayed – ride', 'no luck'– and only serves to make your mother's quest for an ambulance and help more poignant
> I particularly liked your use of a three part list to show how desperate you were to see your brother again.

It is only Trainee 3 who really tries to do exactly what Asif wished:

> You have said 'the body *will* be . . .' but it would make more sense to say 'the body would be . . .' because it is the future conditional tense: 'would have been'.

Although the trainee teachers tried their best with this exercise, they considered it very difficult. Like me, they found that their overwhelming response to this narrative was one of profound human sympathy and respect. They wanted just to leave it to stand as it was, to speak for itself. Trainee 3 is the kindest, most sensitive of teachers: that comment about the future conditional tense quoted above was written with great reluctance in an altruistic attempt to sacrifice her 'frame of reference' for something with which she did not at all feel comfortable.

Befitting emblems of adversity: poetry as a resource

What is the solution? Students like Asif have every right to state their learning requirements and to make claims upon those who teach them. Cox's *adult needs* curriculum model has urgent, legitimate questions to ask of English teachers. We must acknowledge and try to answer those questions in a way that will best help our students advance their precious life chances in a competitive world. If we are committed to practising emotional intelligence in our classrooms, it seems that we are caught in a dilemma. On the one hand, we are urged to try to enter our students' frames of reference, even though they may be very different from our own. On the other hand, we are told that, unless we are first true to ourselves and have a clear understanding of our own core values, we cannot achieve equally vital 'self regulation'. One way out of this apparent impasse might be to consider the principles of Game Theory (Kuhn 1997). Must our encounter be – to use the terminology – 'zero sum' so that one of us only 'wins' if the other 'loses'? Either Asif is forced to talk through his feelings about his brother as if in some compulsory therapy session, wishing all the time that his English teacher would actually teach him to write fluent English, or his teacher is obliged to 'deliver' a reductionist, utilitarian literacy curriculum consisting of a series of decontextualized work-sheets on tenses, apostrophes and spellings? Can we not move – drawing again on the language of Game Theory – to a 'non zero sum' position in which *both* frames of reference are recognized and afforded their due? Our mutual *dyssemia* has caused us both to conceive of the teacher as a *parent* figure – for him, *controlling,* for me, *nurturing.*

Hard as it might seem for those of us committed to *personal growth* to acknowledge, classroom practice which is truly emotionally intelligent requires student and teacher to occupy a very different transactional position: that of the *adult.* Adult behaviour requires intellectual, emotional and moral autonomy. I am not, ultimately, helping Asif if I respond to him in the role of teacher as parent because to do so is just to encourage in him a sense of childish dependency. I cannot accept that an intensely personal, emotionally powerful piece of writing brought into the public space of the English class-room should be treated as if it were nothing more than an opportunity to learn about spelling and tense conventions. To do otherwise is to run the risk of becoming what Abbs predicted with concern over 20 years ago: that 'man carrying a bag of tools but with only other people's jobs to do'. If death is on the mind of this adolescent, then, in a truly emotionally intelligent classroom, its presence must be acknowledged and encountered. On the other hand, there are adult commitments placed on the teacher too: playing the *nurturing parent* role would allow us to evade our responsibilities of looking 'clear-eyed' as it were into the heart of Asif's story. Instead of saying, preciously, that it is beyond assessment or evaluation, we have to try to reconfigure our interpreta-tion of the terms 'affirmation' and 'affiliation' so we can see them from his point of view and find a way of using what he has brought to the classroom as an opportunity to address his adult needs as a writer.

Earlier in the chapter reference was made to Matthew Arnold's affirmation of the power of literature. That power remains as potent today as when Arnold championed it over a century ago; for it is in the imaginative world of the literary text that English teachers committed to emotionally intelligent practice can find accommodation with those who claim their entitlement to an *adult needs* curriculum. When the poet Seamus Heaney (so often, significantly, anthologized for study in the secondary English classroom) felt impelled to address the violence besetting his Irish homeland in the late twentieth century, he framed the question posed by that challenge with a line from Shakespeare's *Sonnet 65*: 'How with this rage shall beauty hold a plea?' And he found his answer in the words of a fellow Irish poet, William Butler Yeats: 'by offering "befitting emblems of adversity"' (Heaney 1980: 57). As a poet who feels a sense of obligation to speak from and of a communal experience, Heaney has searched for symbols which might help those embroiled in such terrible trials to – as John Dixon put it – 'bring order and composure' to their 'inner selves'. Like all poets, Heaney uses what we have heard Goleman call 'the emotional mind's special symbolic modes: metaphor and simile' to achieve this. In a poem like *The Tollund Man,* for example, the peat-preserved body of that sacrificial victim from prehistory helps the narrator to gain some insight into the bloody past of his homeland. On a personal level, too, in *Mid-Term Break* – another poem often taught in the secondary English classroom – the sense of ritual represented by images of poppies, snowdrops and candles 'soothed' not only the bedside but also, perhaps, the grief of the bereaved.

So when Asif brings his story into the public arena of the classroom, my response – one which allows me to remain true to my 'frame of reference' – is to say that we need to explore together the 'special symbolic modes' afforded by poetry. I want Asif to face up, as an adult, to the consequences of his actions. He has chosen to raise a question about the human condition; and in the emotionally intelligent classroom, that question cannot go unanswered. But just as it would be crassly insensitive to dissect, objectively and dispassionately, the tense confusions inherent in his story, so too – as I suggested when I first mentioned *Mid Term Break* earlier in the chapter – would it be to confront Asif immediately with a literary text too painfully close to his personal experience. A more emotionally intelligent way forward might be to find a poem which still creates what Louise Rosenblatt memorably calls a 'live circuit ... between reader and text, (1970: 25) but which also establishes a more fundamental, less personal, meeting point. Staying for our examples with Heaney's much anthologized first collection, *Death of a Naturalist,* I might begin my work with Asif by reading with him a poem like

Blackberry-Picking. This poem does not mention the death of a human being, sudden or otherwise; but in its account of a child's experience of ritual disappointment and the low-key disillusionments of the natural world, it does answer Asif's story by sharing a common awareness of loss and impermanence. By doing so, it allows teacher and student a safe space in which to begin a dialogue, as adult human beings, about things which need to be communicated.

Here is a young trainee teacher reflecting, in a poetry *blog* posting, upon her first encounter with Heaney's poem *Blackberry-Picking* and upon its particular significance for her (Chapter 3 considers in more detail the implications for teaching and learning of the new technologies):

> I think it strikes such a chord with me because it reminds me of my childhood. My Gran and I would walk down the lane near her home to pick blackberries really early in the morning. I'd wear my wellies and carry a large basket which we'd fill to the brim. In the afternoons we'd bake pies and make jam; our hands were all sticky and my tongue was always stained purple by the time my Mum came to take me home. I love Heaney's choice of language, it's so simplistic but very visual. It captures a child's voice so well yet has the interjected [sic] thoughts of a grown man reflecting upon a past memory. By the end of the poem I felt genuine empathy, as I related to the disappointment that I felt as a youngster when the berries turned.

It is interesting to compare this young teacher's comments with Heaney's recollections of his own early experiences of the English poetic canon:

> I also knew the whole of Keats's ode 'To Autumn' but the only line that was luminous then was 'To bend with apples the mossed cottage trees', because my uncle had a small orchard where the old apple trees were sleeved in a soft green moss. (1980: 26)

'Grandmother', 'Uncle': for both, Louise Rosenblatt's 'live circuit' is charged when a connection is established between the experiences articulated in the poem and a resonant familial memory. Once that sympathy has been evoked, the reader becomes alert and receptive to other layers of meaning within the text. Thus, having responded to the pictures painted by Heaney with her own answering image of domestic intimacy, the young trainee teacher is able to engage not only with the language of the poem but also its deeper, darker undertones of impermanence, decay and the passage of time:

> I love Heaney's choice of language, it's so simplistic but very visual. It captures a child's voice so well yet has the interjected thoughts of a grown man reflecting

upon a past memory. By the end of the poem I felt genuine empathy, as I related to the disappointment that I felt as a youngster when the berries turned.

Reflection Activity 2.6

What resources would you turn to, if you wished to plan a lesson which might accommodate Asif's stated learning needs without compromising your own ideals about the nature and purpose of English teaching? Would literature provide a useful way in for you? If so, what text would you choose? If not, what other resources might you consider?

For me, this young trainee teacher's thoughts about *Blackberry-Picking* affirm Matthew Arnold's belief in the power of poetry; and it would be my wish – as a teacher committed to emotionally intelligent practice in my classroom – to guide Asif's encounter with the poem so that he too might be in a position to make a similarly nuanced response, one which moved from personal connection to something more universal. We might begin our exploration by sharing, from our different cultural reference points, personal memories which resonated with what the young trainee teacher described as 'the disappointment . . . felt . . . when the berries turned.' For my part of the story exchange, I might tell Asif, for example, how the magical feeling of anticipation I used to feel as a small child on Christmas Eve, dissipated with the realization that the gifts were actually delivered through a human, rather than supernatural agency. Weaving personal stories around the text in this way allows us to find our own 'befitting emblems of adversity' which, in their turn, offer us a safe way into the issues at the heart of Asif's written account of his brother's death without having, yet, to face the full horror of that event. With time, and talk, and practice and the help of other poems, we can move to a situation where the full force of Asif's tragic experience can be faced with clear-eyed, adult resolution.

To illustrate that point, here are some further comments from the same blog mentioned earlier, in which other trainee teachers reflect on the effect which poetry has had on their lives. In the first example, the respondent is writing about Wilfred Owen's *Dulce Et Decorum Est* – than which it would be hard to imagine a poem more starkly engaged with the horrors of war:

The main reason I chose this poem is that it is the first one that I 'got' in respect of analysing the language and accessing the bigger picture – it is also the one that started me on the journey that has led to become a teacher! In terms of critical analysis – I had an epiphany!

And here is another blog entry, explaining why Elizabeth Bishop's *One Art* has meant so much to the writer:

> I first came across Bishop in a seminar and ended up loving her so much that I ended up doing my undergraduate dissertation on her. I wouldn't say it is the most cheerful poem but it always gets me thinking. At first it seems that the poet is instructing the reader on how to deal with loss but as you read on it becomes obvious that the poet is actually talking about their own pain. The poem is actually their own thoughts and struggles to deal with loss. It may be of interest to know that the poem was written after Bishop's partner committed suicide. Like I said, this poem isn't cheerful but it is a poem which I believe everyone can relate to in some way. We have all experienced loss in some form and I think sometimes it is good to reflect upon those experiences from time to time. After all, they help to shape who we are. Anyway, hope you take a look. Maybe you could let me know what you think.

'I think sometimes it is good to reflect upon those experiences from time to time. After all, they help to shape who we are'. That is the 'frame of reference' which, as a teacher committed to emotionally intelligent practice, the *personal growth* agenda and a determination to conduct my classroom transactions as an *adult* rather than a *controlling parent,* I am not prepared to concede to Asif.

But what about the teacher's part of the bargain? Can an engagement with poetry accommodate Asif's compelling concern that the technical weaknesses of his writing be accommodated? Again, the two quotations cited above suggest a way forward. It is interesting that the trainee teacher who writes about Owen cites her encounter with *Dulce Et Decorum Est* as a moment of conceptual breakthrough so significant that it precipitated a vocational calling. In the same way, the second commentator believes that it was 'loving [Bishop] so much' – and the choice of verb is significant – which caused her to undertake the considerable academic task of writing a dissertation on the poet. Both trainee teachers have been stimulated by their favourite poems to accept what Mortiboys would describe as a decidedly adult challenge which, in its own way, mirrors the challenge undertaken by Owen and Bishop: to craft something powerful, significant and enduring – whether it be a work of art, a career or a dissertation – out of human experience. The verb 'craft' is used purposefully in that last sentence; for if Asif wishes to improve his technical written skills then the way to do so is not to complete an endless round of worksheet exercises but to serve an 'apprenticeship' with the great craftsmen and women of the language. Who better to help Asif reflect upon the effect of time on our lives or the significance of the choices we make about tense endings in our writing than a poet like Philip Larkin? There is *Love Songs in Age,* for example, which poignantly captures a moment in time when a widow, suddenly catching sight of a collection of once familiar but now ageing song books, is transported back to the days of her youth; or *An Arundel Tomb*, which moves from the twentieth century to the medieval period and back again through the centuries in its explorations of the effects of time upon love, endurance and the interpretation of meanings? And if we want to illustrate the power that a carefully chosen tense ending can have, we might think about the way the single word 'Locked' placed at the start of the second verse of *Dockery and Son* and immediately followed by an emphatic full stop, signifies the unbridgeable gap between the protagonist's present and his past.

Asif is a talented writer. To introduce him to the work of other talented writers is to respond to his learning needs as *adult* to *adult,* (to use Mortiboys' terminology) not as *controlling* or even *nurturing parent* to *child.* To place the individual's encounter with powerful imaginative writing at the heart of our classroom practice is to provide a safe communal space in which emotional intelligence can be nurtured and the ties of our common humanity celebrated. By serving a literary apprenticeship in that company (like the girls engaging with *The Winter's Tale* in Chapter 5), we can hone our own skills as speakers and listeners, readers and writers.

3 Ways of Learning

Key Questions

The following key questions underpin the chapter:

1. What practical classroom benefits may be gained from planning activities which take account of the different ways in which students learn?
2. How far can a learning styles approach enhance our awareness of wider educational, social, cultural and political forces at work and promote achievement, diversity and inclusion?
3. Which ways of learning will students need to master in order to operate within the pluralized literacy worlds of the future?
4. How can notions of metacognition and 'learning to learn' enhance students' progress?

The 'learning styles' agenda

As we have seen in Chapters 1 and 2, over the past 30 years or so the concept of learning styles has enabled teachers to review a much wider spectrum of student learning potential than a single definition of 'intelligence'. It is now widely accepted that we all have characteristic preferences and strengths when it comes to absorbing and dealing with new information; the basic idea is that for each individual there are specific settings and circumstances which help them learn better. By the end of the millennium the concept was so firmly embedded that educationalists were likely to think not so much of a student's raw level of 'ability' but rather in terms of his or her possessing a diverse repertoire of competences, preferences and skills which varied according to context; indeed there was a widespread and strongly held belief that teachers should attempt to identify, acknowledge and accommodate their students' different learning styles as a matter of course. This rosy picture becomes rather more complicated, however, when we consider the two comprehensive critiques of the learning styles field conducted by Coffield, Moseley, Hall and Ecclestone in 2004; even after three decades of research, the idea of any unified overarching conceptualized approach appears as futile as Mr Casaubon's quest for the Key to All Mythologies in *Middlemarch*. Although the Coffield team identify 71 learning style models of which 13 are very important in terms of their influence and penetration, there is very little solid evidence-based research upon which to build best practice. Competing researchers with a variety of psychological, sociological, educational and policy-oriented view-points seem to have created more heat than light, while the situation is further complicated by the fact that specific learning styles models have become big business (Coffield et al. 2004a: 54–5).

One of the most popular theories, widely promoted and endorsed by the UK government in the early 2000s, is the modality-specific VAK system of classify-ing strengths and weaknesses. This model (sometimes referred to as Vak or VAKT) suggests that while 'visual' learners respond best to stimuli such as dem-onstrations, pictures or films, 'aural' learners do well with lectures, tapes and podcasts, can follow verbal instructions easily and enjoy speaking and listen-ing, while 'kinaesthetic' and 'tactile' learners prefer physical response activities and work best when they can move around. 'As well as Vak', says Coffield, 'I came across labelling such as "activists" versus "reflectors," "globalists" versus "analysts" and "left brainers" versus "right brainers." There is no scientific justi-fication for any of these terms ... We do students a serious disservice by imply-ing they have only one learning style, rather than a flexible repertoire from which to choose, depending on the context' (Coffield in Henry 2007: 1).

Since the Coffield reports were published we have seen the emergence of an increasing level of dissatisfaction with the learning styles approach. Leading UK neuroscientist Susan Greenfield dismisses the whole idea as 'nonsense', arguing that humans 'have evolved to build a picture of the world through our senses working in unison, exploiting the immense interconnectivity that exists in the brain. It is when the senses are activated together – the sound of a voice is synchronization with the movement of a person's lips – that brain cells fire more strongly than when stimuli are received apart . . . After more than 30 years of educational research into learning styles there is no independent evidence that Vak, or indeed any other learning style inventory, has any direct educational benefits' (Greenfield in Henry 2007: 1). Guy Claxton criticizes the UK government's endorsement of the cause, arguing that the 'language of learning styles has saturated the personalised learning agenda' (Claxton in Revell 2005). John Geake, who has worked extensively on how the human brain processes information, agrees it is wrong to embrace the learning styles approach uncritically. 'We need to take extreme care when moving from the lab to the classroom. We do remember things visually and aurally, but information isn't defined by how it is received. Take the Battle of Trafalgar – you may know the fact, but do you remember how and when you learned it?' (Geake in Revell 2005).

A more practical classroom perspective is expressed by teacher Colin Everest, who sees 'learning styles' as just another stick with which to beat the hapless teacher. 'I am not saying there is nothing of value in the idea that we need to bring a range of approaches and all available resources to bear on getting across important information and ideas,' he argues. 'Nor am I denying that some students find some approaches easier than others because of their previous levels of understanding or other factors. I don't see why, though, I should not be trying to iron out those differences in levels of understanding, bringing all my students in one class to the same point by exposing them all to each one of the relevant influences' (Everest 2003: 1). As Chapter 1 suggested, an oversimplified application of the learning styles approach may, it seems, result in students being allocated an impoverished and restricted set of learning experiences based on little more than a hunch; moreover Carey Jewitt has expressed reservations about the concept when 'being labelled a "visual" or "kinaesthetic" learner appears increasingly to be a code for "low ability"' (Jewitt 2008: 17). When even Alistair Smith, the UK-based pioneer of 'accelerated learning' who sparked much interest in cognitive learning theories nearly 20 years ago, now characterizes VAK as 'one model among many', arguing that the 'brain-based stuff *has a value as metaphor*' (author's emphases), it seems there is a full-scale learning styles backlash under way (Smith in Revell 2005). It is against this problematic background, therefore, when it may seem that spending much time thinking about learning styles is about as productive as rearranging the proverbial deckchairs on the *Titanic*, that the key questions for this chapter are framed.

Learning styles and preferences are largely **constitutionally based** including the four modalities: VAKT[2].	Learning styles reflect deep-seated features of the **cognitive structure**, including 'patterns of ability'.	Learning styles are one component of a relatively **stable personality type**.	Learning styles are **flexibly stable learning preferences**.	Move on from learning styles to **learning approaches, strategies, orientations** and **conceptions of learning**.
Dunn and Dunn[3]	**Riding**	**Apter**	**Allinson and Hayes**	**Entwistle**
Gregorc	Broverman	**Jackson**	**Herrmann**	**Sternberg**
Bartlett	Cooper	**Myers-Briggs**	**Honey and Mumford**	**Vermunt**
Betts	Gardner et al.	Epstein and Meier	**Kolb**	Biggs
Gordon	Guilford	Harrison-Branson	Felder and Silverman	Conti and Kolody
Marks	Holzman and Klein	Miller	Hermanussen,	Grasha-Riechmann
Paivio	Hudson		Wierstra, de Jong and	Hill
Richardson	Hunt		Thijssen	Marton and Säljö
Sheehan	Kagan		Kaufmann	McKenney and Keen
Torrance	Kogan		Kirton	Pask
	Messick		McCarthy	Pintrich, Smith, Garcia
	Pettigrew			and McCeachie
	Witkin			Schmeck
				Weinstein, Zimmerman
				and Palmer
				Whetton and Cameron

Figure 3.1 Families of Learning Styles. *Source:* Coffield et al. 2004a: 46.

It is possible to tie in the Coffield continuum with the age-old nature–nurture debate in that reading from left to right it 'is based on the extent to which the developers of learning styles models and instruments appear to believe that learning styles are fixed' (Coffield et al. 2004a: 20). Thus models such as Gregorc's Style Delineator broadly assume that since pupils' learning styles are stable and genetic, teachers should seek to accommodate them; indeed Gregorc claims that ignoring or working contrary to one's 'Mind Style' may be harmful. Then again, at the opposite end of the spectrum, we find models such as those of Vermunt and Entwistle which challenge us to consider the pedagogical implications of 'personal factors such as motivation and environmental factors like cooperative or individual learning, and also the effects of curriculum design, institutional and course culture and teaching and assessment tasks on how students choose or avoid particular learning strategies' (Coffield et al. 2004b: 10). While the post-age-16 focus of the Coffield study means that there may be somewhat more latitude with regard to curriculum design and assessment than is the case in the age 11 to 16 context, at this end of the Coffield continuum we find a range of ideas which speak persuasively to those of us who believe that taking into account how students learn when planning classroom activities can and does make a difference.

Various learning styles models clearly presuppose different potential pedagogical options and interventions, as Coffield et al. suggest. They point out that 'supporters of fixed traits and abilities argue that a valid and reliable measure is a sound basis for diagnosing individuals' learning needs and then designing specific interventions to address them, both at the level of individual self-awareness and teacher activity' but note that this can be a limiting approach which can leads to student labelling. To avoid this, 'some theorists promote the idea that learners should develop a repertoire of styles, so that an awareness of their own preferences and abilities should not bar them from working to acquire those styles which they do not yet possess' and thus teachers may devise a 'pedagogic sheep dip' to accommodate various learning styles across a scheme of work. Then again, other theorists envisage using 'learning styles instruments as a diagnostic assessment tool that encourages a more self-aware reflection about strengths and weaknesses [and] offers a way for teachers and students to talk more productively about learning, using a more focused vocabulary to do so. Finally, those who reject the idea of learning styles might, nevertheless, see value in creating a more precise vocabulary with which to talk about learning, motivation and the idea of *metacognition* – where better self-awareness may lead to more organized and effective approaches to teaching and learning' (Coffield et al. 2004a: 3). *Metacognition* is revisited in more detail in Chapter 4.

Reflection Activity 3.1

Consider one popular model from Coffield's Families of Learning Styles table (Figure 3.1) which you have come across being applied in a classroom context. What are the potential pros and cons here?

Gardner and Kolb revisited

It was back in the early 1980s when Howard Gardner first suggested an alternative way of measuring learning potential by proposing in *Frames of Mind* a pluralized concept of seven 'multiple intelligences' – linguistic, spatial, logical-mathematical, musical, bodily kinaesthetic, interpersonal and intrapersonal – to which he later added two more types, naturalist and existential (Gardner 1983). As Knud Illeris argues, Gardner's 'limited, clear and relatively easily comprehended' model 'lets the air out of the one-dimensional branding and at times also elitist-oriented thinking' that had often characterized it (Illeris 2007: 181). Logically, therefore, the school 'should be a place where there is room enough to cultivate the intelligences that the individual child is good at, and provide it with support to be capable of managing reasonably well in the other areas' (Illeris 2007: 181). As Carey Jewitt notes, Gardner's ideas still seem relevant with regard to 'issues of inclusion and social justice, the need to respect diversity, to engage with the abilities of all students, to personalize learning, and the need to provide a broad and rich curriculum that motivates and connects with students' interests' (Jewitt 2008: 15). Teachers want to believe that children are good at different things and show them that their aptitudes are valued; as teacher Philip Beadle has commented, MI theory is 'an immensely seductive measure for those of us working with students who find areas of the curriculum difficult to access. Helping a student to discover what they are good at and giving this the term "intelligence" can have a marked effect on their self-esteem,' yet as he goes on to point out, if misapplied, 'MI can be used to deny the need to work at things. And, as such, can end up being just as reductive a form of labelling as the previous forms its application in schools seeks to overthrow' (Beadle 2006a).

The charge of stereotyping has also been levelled at David Kolb's influential experiential learning model, which is founded upon the belief that people receive information in different ways (concretely or abstractly) and go on to use it differently too (actively or reflectively). Illeris argues that this may be seen 'yet another example of Kolb's mastery in putting everything in its place in his system and thereby quite firmly limiting and systematising human diversity' (Illeris 2007: 186). This potential narrowing or self-limiting aspect of learning styles theory is, indeed, one to guard against. As Illeris points out, 'the concept concerning learning styles seems, to an even higher degree than the intelligence concept, to lead to the learning situation having to be adapted to some fixed characteristics of the learners and thus to overlook the fact that the learners can change and develop on the basis of the challenges that they meet or are faced with' (Illeris 2007: 187). Indeed, while some children seem to adapt so effortlessly to different types of task that the learning styles issue never comes up, for others there does seem to be a lag between their actual level of ability and the work they produce in specific contexts. Left unchallenged, there is a risk of a consequent (and understandable) reluctance to engage with a key aspect of the curriculum developing which can be demotivating and debilitating.

Motivation, often linked to self-esteem, plays an important role in creating and sustaining the concentration everyone needs to learn effectively; this is clearly strongly related to Daniel Goleman's notion of emotional intelligence, which will be discussed in detail in the following chapter of this book. Psychologist Mogens Hansen suggests that 'without targeted attention, i.e. will-directed, focused and enduring attention, one learns nothing. . . . Will-directed attention is part of directing function of the brain and the conscious-ness, called the executive function, which is used for the self-regulation of actions on the basis of intentionality . . . planning and decisions. . . . Those who do not learn anything are the same as those who have never learned to control their own attention' (Hansen 2005: 28–9 in Illeris 2007: 183). As suggested in Chapters 1 and 2, if students unwilling or unable to focus on their learning cannot learn, we must offer a range of activities to engage their attention which are relevant to their future goals and demonstrably worthy of attention; a learning styles model proven to raise levels of achievement would clearly be of enormous benefit in such a task. This is where Kolb's ideas still seem poten-tially relevant, for as well as reminding us to provide a range of activities and strategies appropriate for the specific work set, he also provides some practical insights into the ways in which we may need to adopt various pedagogic roles during different stages of a lesson sequence.

Kolb described those who learn best by being involved in an experience (Concrete Experience), by watching, listening and reflecting (Reflective Observation) and by thinking (Abstract Conceptualization) and by doing (Active Experimentation); his model looks at how students take in new infor-mation and then manage it, and he suggests learners use all four processes but often favour some over others. Working with Kolb's taxonomy can make us think carefully about a range of teaching approaches we might use to cater for learners with different strengths and weaknesses: he suggests four roles for the teacher to be effective with different types of learner – communicator of information, guide or taskmaster, coach or helper, and role model (Kolb 2000: 17). Students and teachers bring to the table a range of skills, experiences, levels of confidence, needs and expectations which shape the learning environment and often shift roles in different contexts; to manage learning effectively teachers might play a variety of roles, from devil's advocate or agent provocateur to neutral manager or committed ally, to help students think more critically and analytically. It may well be worth bearing in mind this notion of teaching 'roles' when you come to read the section of Chapter 4 of this book which discusses the importance of purposeful classroom talk.

Thus, although none of the currently popular competing theories carries any scientific endorsement, even if considering the ways in which students learn does little more than remind us that they are all individuals with their own personalities, it has still done much. Indeed, in thinking through how an awareness of the multiple ways in which students acquire and process information can help us to teach more effectively, it is worth quoting Gardner himself:

> So long as materials are taught and assessed in only one way, we will only reach a certain kind of child. But everything can be taught in several ways. The more we can match youngsters to congenial approaches of teaching, learning and assessing, the more likely it is that those youngsters will achieve educational success. (Gardner in Beadle 2006a)

Case Study: Melanie tells her own story

The pedagogical context for this chapter is 14-year-old Melanie's attempts to describe a significant personal experience both orally and in writing. Both versions of her narrative are reproduced in the following pages.

Thinking of a topic is no problem for Melanie, who knows what types of text she has to produce and how her work will be assessed. Like Asif, whose story lay at the heart of Chapter 2 of this book, Melanie has chosen her own subject matter and seizes the opportunity to communicate a profoundly powerful personal experience. In terms of speaking and listening, she will give an 'individual extended contribution' which accesses the UK AQA examination board's 'explain, describe, narrate'

⇨

Case Study—Cont'd

triplet for talk. The relevant assessment criteria require her to 'communicate clearly and imaginatively, structuring and sustaining . . . talk and adapting it to different situations, using standard English appropriately'; to 'participate in discussion by both speaking and listening, judging the nature and purposes of contributions and the roles of participants'; and to 'adopt roles and communicate with audiences using a range of techniques'. The other part of her task involves writing to 'imagine, explore, entertain', and here Melanie should 'communicate clearly and imaginatively, using and adapting forms for different readers and purposes' and 'organise ideas into sentences, paragraphs and whole texts using a variety of linguistic and structural features'. Yet her learning needs to offer her something beyond a few more marks she can eventually cash in for a paper qualification, however necessary that may be: it should also prepare her for a world of multiple literacies in which she has access to a range of discourses and media undreamt of by previous generations. Beyond this, however, working through these tasks can help Melanie identify how she learns best and think about ways in which to diversify her strategies as she works with these very different modalities of English in order to prepare for her future as (hopefully) a lifelong learner.

This brave new world of multiple literacies was anticipated by Gunther Kress in *Writing the Future* (1995) when he sought to 'map out the terrain for the new debate' about the place of English within the curriculum amid a 'changing landscape of communication' (Kress 1995: 94). More recently there has emerged, as Richard Andrews puts it,

> a growing awareness that schooling and curriculum are losing touch with the real contexts in which learning takes place. The drivers behind the changing landscape for learning include an increasing access for families to multimedia and the internet in the home; the gradual disappearance of the idea of 'education' as being a separate bolt-on dimension for cultural institutions, but rather it becoming a central part of their identity and function; a dissatisfaction among parents and children with conventional teaching techniques designed to gain maximum results for the school in its fight to rise up the league tables of performance; and changing literacies (e.g. the creation of websites by children and young people) which are not recognised within the formal curriculum. (Andrews 2001: 15)

Interestingly, Andrews sees England and Wales as behind other countries 'in their slowness in recognising the value of real-world experiences to inspire and inform literacy development' (Andrews 2001: 15). It is against this backdrop, then, that we must evaluate the opportunities we are providing for students like Melanie as we set up, support and evaluate their learning.

Here, then, is the first draft of Melanie's written autobiographical account:

<u>My Operation</u>

As I was sat nervously in the waiting room, I didn't really know what was going on. Why had I just had x-rays? Was something wrong with me? I was too young at the time to know the answers to those questions, and looking back, I'm sure no seven-year-old would.

I was diagnosed at seven with Ideopathic Scoliosis. This means that I had a curved spine and the doctors didn't know what had caused this.

As I grew up, my spine became more twisted and curved. Also as I grew taller the pain became worse too.

At the age of twelve, my consultant decided to do an operation on my spine because it was getting out of control. What did I feel when he told me? Shock. Fear. Relief?

The operation was in two stages: Firstly, anterior and multiple disectomy via the right thoracotomy. This basically means that they took out a rib from the right side and used it as a bone graft on my spine. Then they tried to twist my ribcage back into place because it had been twisted out of shape as my spine had curved.

Secondly, posterior instrumental correction of scoliosis. This ment that my spine was straightened up and fused after the cartalige was removed from the top few vertebrae. Then they put two titanium rods down either side of my spine, then screwed them into place so that it ended up looking like I had a metal ladder across my spine.

The operation took ten and a half hours to complete, ten days in hospital and six weeks at home. It left a scar the length of my spine down my back and a scar across my side seven inches long. It was extremely painful and even after a year it still aches. I couldn't play any sport for a year or ride my bike, but I was allowd to go swimming to help my muscles regrow back strongly where they had been sliced.

I am happy I had this operation because apart from scars my back is normal and it made me realise that my friends and family will always be there for me.

This is a transcript of the oral presentation Melanie produced on the basis of her writing. It was accompanied by an illustrated PowerPoint and several sound and music clips which are indicated in italics:

This is my prepared talk and PowerPoint on my operation.

So what was the problem? When I was only seven, I was diagnosed with thoracic idiopathic scoliosis. This meant that I had a curved spine in the

⇨

Case Study—Cont'd

shape of an 'S'. This is because as I grew taller my bones were pushed in a different direction than what would be normal. Then as I grew up the curve became more noticeable and more painful. Last year my surgeon decided to operate before my spine got so twisted he wouldn't be able to fix it at all.

This is an X-ray of my back before my surgery. *[Photograph]*

Like all operations it had some of its own risks. *[Music Clip: 'Jaws' shark attack theme]* I was warned the operation would take ten and a half hours and afterwards I would be in a lot of pain and flat on my back in a high-dependency hospital bed for nine days and there was a very slight risk of ending up in a wheelchair or even dead. I was understandably very scared and very frightened, but I was still one of the lucky ones. In the olden days scoliosis was often fatal. People would suffocate as the pressure from their twisted ribcage eventually crushed their lungs, which would have been slow and very painful.

The last thing I remember before I went to sleep from the anaesthetic was Mr Rao, my surgeon, smiling at me as the anaesthetic started to work, holding a gigantic metal saw. *[Music Clip: 'Psycho' shower scene theme]* Either he was about to start carving a turkey, or . . . Well, luckily that's when I fell asleep – thank God!

My surgery – part one – was anterior and multiple discectomy via right thoracotomy. While I was on my side, they cut through my ribcage on the right side and removed a rib to use as a bone graft on my spine. *[Sound Clip: loud chainsaw]* Next they took out the cartilage, which is the soft spongy jelly filling between the top few discs of my spine, to make it straighter. As you can imagine it was extremely painful. My surgery – part two – was posterior instrumental correction of scoliosis. I was then turned onto my stomach and sliced open from the top to the base of my spine. Finally two thin titanium rods were placed either side of my spine and then bolted together like a ladder to straighten my back. So that was also as painful, if not more, than my first stage.

This is my fused spine with all the metalwork, after surgery. *[Photograph]*

The first thing I remember when I woke up was I could not open my eyes at all and I felt really spaced out and I had no spatial awareness at all. I asked for my dad but he wasn't allowed into the recovery room at first, so I cried my eyes out and then went back to sleep. The next time I woke up it was the middle of the night, seven hours later. That's when the pain started, and stayed for a very long time!

Then I discovered, sticking in and out of me, drains in my back and my side to allow blood, plasma and other liquids to drip out of the wounds. An anaesthetic drip of painkillers. A hand-held clicker so that I could top up my morphine for extra pain relief when I needed it rigged up so I could only get the drug every 5 minutes so I couldn't overdose! Tubes in my neck and wrists so that medicines could be injected straight into my veins, because I couldn't lift my head to swallow anything. Stylish knee socks to help my circulation while I was stuck in bed. A catheter, which is a wee tube, to drain my . . . well, work it out for yourselves!

This is me before I woke up after my surgery, not looking my best. *[Photograph]*

The results were that the doctors said that it was one of the best corrections they had ever seen. I had lost nearly twelve pounds in weight because I didn't eat for about a week. Also my stomach had shrunk as a result of this, because I hadn't eaten anything. My sister said I looked like a skeleton. I grew from being 5 feet 2 inches tall to 5 feet 6 inches overnight!

Well you're probably wondering what happened next. I was off school for six weeks and had a home tutor. I was banned from sport for a year. My scar faded to a thin silver line. I went on holiday to Egypt and Tunisia, where I was able to swim, surf a bit and even go parasailing without any pain at all, so it was well worth while.

This is a picture of me doing a bit of surfing in the swimming pool in Tunisia. *[Photograph and Music Clip: 'Hawaii 5–0' theme]*

This picture is of me and my dad parasailing on top of the Mediterranean Sea. *[Photograph]*

Was it all worthwhile? Although I couldn't do sport for a year, it is much less painful now I've started playing hockey and running again. My out-of-line ribcage has become less noticeable and is only slightly curved now. My crooked spine is now the straightest of anyone I know, so yes, it was definitely worth it.

In the future I could have another operation, but it is not for my health. It is completely cosmetic. It is also to flatten my ribs and improve the appearance of my back. I have to be at least 19 years old for this and it is completely my choice – it is not up to my parents to decide for me. I am not sure if I want to do this because it involves breaking all my ribs and bending them into the right shape, which is even more painful than what I have already had done – but my back would look better. So maybe I will – maybe I won't. I have plenty of time to decide. All I know is that it will be a very tough choice.

Reflection Activity 3.2

Before assessing Melanie's two narratives using Geoff Petty's 'atomistic' knife, to engage fully with an account of such a life-changing personal experience also requires you to don his 'holistic' pair of spectacles, as discussed in Chapter 1 of this book. Think, too, of the notion of emotional intelligence which underpins the story of Asif in Chapter 2 and consider both the Melanie behind these texts as their creator and the Melanie within them as the protagonist.

In Chapter 1 of this book Richard Andrews' model of the writing code (2001) was used to compare the work of Mark and Natalie; here we can use specific levels of this taxonomy to analyse Melanie's writing in Vygotskian terms to locate her Zone of Proximal Development as well as comparing aspects of it with her oral account. At the basic grapho-phonemic level, for instance, while Melanie's left-handed writing is clear and often cursive, the backward slant and the unusual formation of the letter 'a' are likely to slow her down. She also needs to practise some alternative spelling strategies; given her substitution of *ment* for *meant*, perhaps a visual strategy such as looking at linked words like *mean* and *meaning* would help. An aural approach might correct her confusion of *aloud* for *allowed*: a mnemonic such as 'I hear *a loud* sound when someone shouts *aloud*', for instance; then again, looking at suffixes and regular past tense verb formations could do the same job in this case. Different types of spelling challenge obviously demand different learning approaches.

Lexically we might wish to encourage Melanie to use a much wider range of imaginative adjectives and adverbs. Syntactically she needs help with sentencing and paragraphing for effect; the opening of her written account is fluent and gripping as she creates pace and tension through a variety of sentence types and a series of effective questions which build rapport with the audience, but before long one-sentence paragraphs become monotonous and there is only a rather sparse factual description of the surgery – 'they took out a rib from the right side and used it as a bone graft on my spine.' Note how much less vivid this description is that in Melanie's spoken version; 'they took out the cartilage, which is the soft spongy jelly filling . . . I was then turned onto my stomach and sliced open from the top to the base of my spine.' Textually and contextually, the initial structural impact of atmospheric flashbacks, quick-fire questions and hindsight is not sustained here; the remorselessly chronological approach could be cross-cut much more effectively, and the conclusion feels rather clichéd and anticlimactic.

In contrast, though the spoken version begins rather blandly and is characteristically dialogic in form, Melanie soon begins to speak inventively, fluently and with a finely judged sense of pace which leads to a moving cliff-hanger ending. Lexically she juxtaposes high-register medical jargon such as 'thoracotomy' and 'discectomy' with more down-to-earth vocabulary in both versions, but it is only in the spoken version that she counterbalances 'catheter' and 'wee tube' so effectively. Textually, lists are used in the spoken version to further ratchet up narrative tension and create a montage effect in which humour leavens the seriousness of the subject; 'drains in my back and my side to allow blood, plasma and other liquids to drip out of the wounds.

An anaesthetic drip of painkillers. A hand-held clicker so that I could top up my morphine for extra pain relief. . . . Tubes in my neck and wrists so that medicines could be injected straight into my veins, because I couldn't lift my head to swallow anything. Stylish knee socks to help my circulation while I was stuck in bed. A catheter, which is a wee tube, to drain my . . . well, work it out for yourselves!' Contextually, Melanie manipulates the autobiographical genre in original and interesting ways in her spoken narrative, moving easily between a historical perspective and her own contemporary experience; 'I was understandably very scared and very frightened, but I was still one of the lucky ones. In the olden days scoliosis was often fatal. People would suffocate as the pressure from their twisted ribcage eventually crushed their lungs.' Very briefly, then, we have summarized Melanie's work here, but it is arguably in the crucial area of metacognition that we can plan for learning most productively using the learning styles approach.

Metacognition and the new literacies

Describing the writing process, Melanie says, 'there are too many things to think about. What you want to say, spelling, paragraphs, all the stuff like that. But when you're speaking, you can use notes to remind you, but it's not like a script because you can still say what you want.' As Andrews observes, distinguishing between composition and transcription 'separates two aspects of writing that can muddle the writer if conflated, often causing a "writing block" because the attention is on the surface when it should be on the deeper features of the composition' (Andrews 2001: 42). Melanie's personal stake in her topic is crucial in terms of Arnold's model of writing development, which focuses upon process more than product and explores 'the powerful psychological benefits which accrue from feeling centred in one's own exploratory writing and focusing on one's expressive needs' (Arnold 1991 in Andrews 2001: 43). When planning her writing and speaking Melanie needs to know that there is a real audience and purpose for her work beyond the demands of any form of external assessment. Heightening her awareness of communicating with an audience – either contemporaneously and face-to-face via speech, or temporally and spatially separated in written form – can illuminate the two-way dialogic processes of speaking and listening *and* writing and reading and thus help Melanie achieve an enhanced metacognitive sense of her own abilities as a maker of meaning. While there are certainly writing skills to be practised and consolidated here, we would not wish to neglect the valuable opportunities for self-actualization and self-expression which are also present. Indeed, as Arnold suggests:

> Self-reflection and reflexiveness are fundamental to self-development and the personalisation of knowledge. Writing can play a part in the development of creative, integrated human beings who can afford to respect the uniqueness of themselves and of others because they have experienced their own capacity to make a mark in the world. (Arnold 1991 in Andrews 2001: 44)

Perhaps, as Tom Crick, the tragic narrator of Graham Swift's *Waterland*, suggests, man really is 'the story-telling animal. He has to go on telling stories, he has to keep making them up. As long as there's a story, it's all right' (Swift 1992: 62–3). As a story-teller, then, Melanie now has to bridge the gap between the complex and interesting ideas she can express orally and her ability to convey these in writing, when transcriptional and compositional aspects pose a particular challenge.

As an effective collaborative learner who gains much from asking questions and volunteering answers, receiving peer feedback on her speech could allow Melanie to transfer her increasing metacognitive knowledge about effective oral communication into a written context. In order to increase students' knowledge about the four modalities of the English curriculum, 'since language development depends on their interrelatedness, [our] teaching needs to build on the links between them' (DfEE 1999a: 6 in Andrews 2001: 13). Currently, however, as surely as connecting 'speaking and listening' foregrounds the essential symbiosis between the two, separating 'reading' and 'writing' masks their reciprocal links. In learning that speaking well can help her to write better, Melanie can develop an ear (and then an eye) for how sentences sound (and then look) when fluently paced and structured. Reading her work aloud can help her spot errors such as the classic 'comma splice' when it becomes apparent that the pause she has indicated has little impact. As Andrews notes, punctuation is 'a surface feature or skill determined by the ability to think in and structure sentences. In other words, it is hard to know how to punctuate unless you know what you want to say and how you want to say it' (Andrews 2001: 53). Speaking before writing (and perhaps recording that speech) does away with many of the inhibitions and tensions young writers experience because much of the composition can be done in advance of the transcription process.

Even though she was not instructed to do so, Melanie chose to structure her spoken discourse around a sequence of sound clips, visual images and bitesized chunks of written text; this decision can be used to scaffold further metacognitive reflection upon the nature and purpose of the narrative modes with which she has worked. The educational context in which Melanie is working, experimenting with a hybrid model of communicative practice in which she simultaneously uses (and expects her audience to use) verbal, visual and audial forms, is in effect redrawing the boundaries of the traditional primarily linguistic English curriculum to encompass a much more diverse worldwide version. Nowadays, as Carey Jewitt notes, theorists like Gunter Kress have taken 'an increased interest in the role of the visual in children's learning, with growing recognition of its potential for engaging learners with the visual aspects of writing and reading, as well as students' production of multimodal models and digital multimedia materials' (Jewitt 2008: 20). As well as linguistic and verbal literacies, today's students need to develop digital, critical and visual literacies which enable them to source, interpret and mediate many different types of text. They need appropriate methodologies with which to manage the enormous ungated knowledge sources available to them via the Internet. Thinking about ways in which our present-day classroom practice can future-proof English presents an undeniable challenge to teachers' professional identities, traditions and practices. The ongoing mass digitization of texts and the emergence of new modes of reading are already transforming the modern English classroom; as Jewitt remarks, 'speech and writing are enmeshed with images, photographs, video excerpts downloaded from the Internet, illustrations in anthologies and novels, teacher drawings on whiteboards, as well as the images, sound, music and animation used in DVDs and CD-ROMS. Digital video – easily accessed via internet connected interactive whiteboards (IWBs) – is increasingly used . . . and has been found to support students' writing and awareness of narrative structures in a medium that young people use in their everyday experiences' (Jewitt 2008: 20, Reid 2003). IWBs allow pupils to manipulate texts, sounds and images and incorporate them into new texts in new ways. A generation ago Adrian Henri mixed two widely different source texts, Wordsworth's iconic Romantic poem and a Dutch car advertisement, to create the found poem *The New, Fast, Automatic Daffodils;* the technology now exists to take this idea to a new level.

As Andrews argues, multimedia technology enables use to move 'between many more different channels of communication – speech, music, images (still and moving), text – and between different genres and forms' (Andrews 2001: 125). Having researched the medical details of her surgery on the Internet, Melanie then uses her sources actively and creatively, editing and manipulating them rather than passively cutting and pasting; further collaborative work in this digital space could consolidate the link between reading and writing. Contributing to the design of a scoliosis website aimed at young people of her own age would be likely to generate the kind of collaborative student talk around creating a digital text noted by Richard Andrews, 'sharply focused on the details of composition, from the arrangement of the text, the style and register in which it was written and its content, to surface features such as spelling and punctuation' (Andrews 2001: 123). Rather than being hidebound by restrictive notions about VAK, therefore, perhaps we should work with what Carey Jewitt calls a 'pluralised notion of literacy and teaching, which draws on a variety of forms of representation and communication' (Jewitt 2008: 56). Since students need to be able to access a range of learning strategies to make sense of this new world, it is, as Carey Jewitt suggests:

> increasingly important for education to attend to the literacy practices of students and the diverse ways of making meaning, in particular the multilingual, visual and multimodal, and the digital. In short, there is a need to approach literacy practices as an inter-textual web of contexts and technology, rather than isolated sets of skills and competences. (Jewitt 2008: 56)

To meet the twenty-first-century learning needs of our students, we need to see the classroom as a shared creative space in which they can work with as wide a range of the new print and digital text types as possible in order to narrow the gap between the traditional narrowly linguistic definition of literacy which has always dominated educational practice and the developing multimodal literacies our pupils now encounter in the wider world.

Melanie is beginning to unite school-based and out-of-school contexts for learning by drawing upon the visual and linguistic literacies she has developed through using social networking sites such as MSN and Facebook; this suggests that, as Howard Gardner argues, 'intelligence' is transferable and allows the student to solve problems across a variety of cultural settings. Now Melanie is capable of analysing aspects of the relationship between the producer and the receiver of a text she would no doubt benefit from posting future examples of her writing on a young writers' website, blog or wiki (via Intranet or Internet) to facilitate peer review and feedback, thus further broadening the contexts for classroom literacy. Similarly, students struggling to remember the multifarious details of a complex nineteenth-century novel might design Facebook profile pages for the key characters or summarize the events of each chapter in 140 character microblog 'tweets', as modelled by Aciman and Rensin in *Twitterature* (2009). Carey Jewitt describes a project in a Soweto secondary school which stemmed from 'the literacy worlds of the students, infused with many different languages, cultures, music and performance not usually heard or seen in the classroom. These literary worlds provided the focus for poetry writing for the design and production of an anthology. The use of performance and visual arts opened up the voices of students who were identified as 'reluctant writers' (Jewitt 2008: 23). The resources and technologies teachers have access to today offer immense possibilities in terms of teaching and learning, allowing us to celebrate within our classrooms the personal, social and cultural lives of our pupils while simultaneously finding ways in which, as Carey Jewitt suggests, 'the visual and multimodal can bring young people into a productive relationship with writing' (Jewitt 2008: 23).

Reflection Activity 3.3

Consider one way in which the boundaries of 'classroom literacy' could be extended using technology. What are the challenges associated with your chosen approach? How might they be overcome?

Bernstein's sociology of pedagogy and the learning styles agenda

Before going on to analyse Melanie's work in detail, let us pause to consider the crucial extent to which thinking about the ways in which individuals learn can raise our awareness of how certain educational and pedagogical practices replicate patterns of social inequality. In *Pedagogy, Symbolic Control and Identity* (1996), Basil Bernstein argues:

> A school metaphorically holds up a mirror in which an image is reflected. There may be several images, positive and negative. A school's ideology may be seen as a construction in a mirror through which images are reflected. The question is: who recognises themselves as of value? What other images are excluded by the dominant image of value so that some students are unable to recognise themselves? In the same way, we can ask about the acoustic of the school. Whose voice is heard? Who is speaking? Who is hailed by the voice? For whom is it familiar? (1996: 7)

Bernstein's sociology of pedagogy suggests that the ways in which society itself configures and contextualizes models of power and control necessarily filter into the context of the school. Furthermore, not only is 'an unequal distribution of images, knowledges, possibilities and resources which will affect the rights of participation, inclusion and individual enhancement of groups of students' but these excluded students will come from disadvantaged social backgrounds (Bernstein 1996: 8). How, Bernstein asks, does the school contend with the problematic interface between the outside world and 'the hierarchies of knowledge, possibility and value' promoted within it? The school does that largely through creating and maintaining a fiction or 'mythological discourse' which attempts to iron out social inequalities by generating 'horizontal solidarities' to challenge the differential power possessed by different social groups beyond the school gates (Bernstein 1996: 9). As Coffield et al. suggest, thinking about ways of learning can perhaps begin to bridge the gap between the personal and the political by encouraging us to consider not only the milieux in which learning takes place but also the nature, relevance and purpose of that learning in the first place (Coffield et al. 2004a: 51). Learning styles theorists such as Entwistle and Vermunt 'have shown that attention needs to be given not only to individual differences in learners, but to the whole teaching–learning environment. Both have demonstrated that while the motivations, self-representations, metacognitive and cognitive strengths and weaknesses of learners are all key features of their learning style, these are also a function of the systems in which learners operate' (Coffield et al. 2004a: 38). As Bernstein puts it:

> some social groups are aware that schooling is not neutral, that it presupposes familial power both material and discursive, and that such groups use this knowledge to improve their children's pedagogic success. It may be that they have to rationalise their children's success by believing that their children deserve such success while others do not. (1996: 9)

This 'familial power' can take many forms, from the purely financial (being able to afford private school fees, buying a home in the catchment area of a high-achieving state-maintained school or hiring a private tutor, for instance) to the more subtly 'discursive'. Whereas some children have educationally and culturally well-capitalized parents ideally placed to secure the educational entitlement of their own offspring, others, manifestly, do not. Perhaps, therefore, we should be mindful that a decontextualized or simplistic focus on individual learning styles which reframes students' failure to learn as their teachers' failure to teach properly may obscure a wider debate about the extent to which educational inequalities are embedded in social and cultural structures which are unlikely to be easily rectified. While in no sense a panacea for these apparently intractable inequalities of opportunity, it is at least possible that in bringing new and enhanced visual, audial, kinaesthetic and tactile ways of learning into the classroom, the new technologies can enhance our awareness of ways in which to expand the horizons of all students rather than only those of the already privileged.

Another way in which teachers may try to generate Bernstein's 'horizontal solidarities' is, of course, to think in terms of MI theory; we want to let our students know we value their individual talents and achievements and Gardner has given us a way of articulating this. Yet in the wider world, beyond the classroom, there are few careers which allow us to simply opt out of receiving or processing information in ways we don't much like. If we think again of Bernstein's powerful analogy of the school as holding up a mirror in which students see various images of themselves reflected, we can see that one reason students from socially disadvantaged backgrounds are less likely to succeed academically is that they tend to view themselves as poor learners. Thus, the onus is on teachers to equip *all* students with the tools they need to identify, develop and value their personal learning strengths and aptitudes in order to prepare for future educational opportunities. At present, as Knud Illeris has noted, international 'lifelong learning' programmes are hugely affected by the 'so-called "Matthew effect" that "for whoever has to him shall be given and he shall be caused to be in abundance" (Matthew 13: 12), that is, those who already are the best educated participate in adult education programmes to a considerable greater extent than those with brief schooling' (Illeris 2007: 195).

Metacognition in practice: Melanie makes plans for future learning

If we think again of Jonothan Neelands' key questions for teachers (mentioned in Chapter 1 of this book), it is clear that trying to teach each student exclusively according to his or her individual preferences (even if there were any scientifically proven method of ascertaining these in the first place) is far less productive than planning a variety of tasks and activities which offer appropriate levels of stretch and challenge for all. While it is often possible to accommodate a variety of activities during process work – the 'circuit training' idea largely based upon Gardner's MI theory – this approach may be impossible when the product, modality or outcome itself is being assessed, as with Melanie's work here. The traditional transcription process offers little by way of visual, audial, musical or kinaesthetic stimulus; Melanie says 'when you're talking people can point out then and there what you have done wrong, or if they can't follow you, but in writing you can't tell what they're thinking while they're reading it because there's no eye contact or feedback. You only know afterwards, not as you're going along.' She knows that writing provides no contemporaneous shared communication context or talk space; feedback may comprise a brief commentary on her written draft received some time later. Yet the very circumstances that can promote learning for some students may be less appropriate for others. Other learners may find oral work as fearful as Melanie finds it reassuring precisely because of that lack of distance between speaker and audience which she values; the very last thing a shyer child wants to witness is instant feedback from their peers. Nevertheless, helping students to recognize their own learning preferences and to consider those of others metacognitively – talking about learning, in other words – can be used as a 'motivational "ice-breaker," as a means of "warming up" the class, or as an activity-based introduction to the topic of learning', as Coffield suggests (Coffield et al. 2004a: 38).

In this context, an effective starter activity might use the multi-modal VAK model to demonstrate how a speech can be made to appeal to a diverse audience if it incorporates images, music and movement. Creating this kind of 'lexicon of learning for dialogue' (Coffield 2004a: 38) allows students to discuss their initial thoughts about how to structure a talk with their teacher and peers and then take steps to develop their ideas further *before the performance*. For Melanie, the next step would be to apply this enhanced level of critical self-awareness to the production of her writing, thus improving her subject knowledge while also thinking about how to extend her current repertoire of learning skills. This level of metacognition can prevent the phenomenon of 'learned helplessness' (which will be discussed further in Chapter 5) and encourage both students and teachers to select a way of working matched to the task, as opposed to the other way round. The aim of the task must be central to the learning method(s) used. Of course it can be very hard to get students to move outside their learning comfort zone; here, then, is a genuine classroom challenge.

On the basis of her learning experience here, Melanie begins to plan for the future. In this instance she chose to write first and then use this as the basis for her talk, but next time she wants to reverse this:

> If I did the speaking part first next time I think it might be better because it's more creative. You don't have to worry so much about your writing skills because you can use pictures and music instead. With a PowerPoint you can have bullet points to help you remember your main points and then when you write it up later you would have a paragraph plan for your essay and in the links between the facts you could focus on getting your English right then because you wouldn't be worried

about not having anything good to write. If you could look back on your speech you might be able to write in a more relaxed way and get a creative feel for it. Looking back now, I think writing about my operation first meant I concentrated on facts too much and not enough on making it interesting for the reader, so it ended up more like a report. So next time I'd speak first, but only if I was allowed to use a PowerPoint, because the pictures and the bullet points remind you of what you want to say.

Here Melanie reveals not only an explicit awareness of the fact that the modalities of speech and writing are very different but also an encouraging awareness of some of the ways in which her oral presentation can be used to ease the transition from her preferred communication mode into a less favoured one. Whereas speech is ephemeral and can make use of paralanguage and instant feedback, writing is fixed and must allow for the producer and receiver of the text to be geographically or temporally distant from each other. Having identified this key generic difference, Melanie might go on to improve her written accuracy by reading her draft aloud. She has already included music and still images in this talk; next time she might incorporate relevant moving-image clips appropriately sourced from the Internet to capture her audience's attention. In terms of the kinaesthetic dimension, I have observed students demonstrating how to tack up and groom a horse, cast a fishing line, serve overarm in tennis, perform basic ballet steps, French-braid a friend's hair and communicate in sign language: in each case, the activity allowed them to think about how the techniques speakers use to engage an audience are similar to and different from the techniques used to interest a reader. Furthermore, while it is impossible to substitute a picture or a sound file for a paragraph when it is the written text itself which is being assessed, students can still investigate some of the ways in which writers try to replicate visual images and soundscapes in words, since a multisensory appeal is often a feature of powerful imaginative writing.

Case Study: Laura reads *The Lady of Shalott*

This case study shows some of the problems which can occur when students are not fully engaged in managing and understanding their own learning. Here 18-year-old Laura recalls her experience of English in the early years of secondary education:

> I remember being really excited when we were told we would be studying Tennyson's *The Lady of Shalott*. I was about 12 I think. I read the poem

Case Study—Cont'd

before we started it in class and because English was my favourite subject, I was really keen to learn the proper way to write a grown-up essay but the lessons just did not suit the way I wanted to work. Looking back, I can see that my class was difficult; there were quite a few kids with special needs and behavioural issues and some people who were struggling because English was not their first language. But I hated the group work and couldn't see why I had to do group work like drawing maps of Shalott and doing freeze-frames instead of studying the poem properly. I just got bored and quite disillusioned with English. After a while I pretty much switched off in lessons.

Reflection Activity 3.4

Read Laura's story (above) and assess the probable learning aims and objectives of her teacher. How might the learning styles approach used here have been managed more effectively?

Ways of learning then and now

In her poignant autobiography *The Great Western Beach* Emma Smith recalls the two very different women who taught her and her sister Pam during the late 1920s and early 1930s. Mrs Oliver is such a disaster that the two girls resort to teaching themselves and discover the 'secret pleasure' of poetry with its 'magical property of banishing boredom'. Adopting a winningly independent repertoire of visual, audial and kinaesthetic independent learning strategies, Pam and Ellie 'save [themselves] from the stultifying dreariness of her inept ministrations':

The last of the poetic sagas we discover – the hardest for us to learn by heart, but the most exciting – is *The Pied Piper of Hamelin*. We are enraptured by this richly moral folk tale: '*Come in, said the Mayor, looking bigger / And in did come the strangest figure* . . .' Oh, the huge drama of it! '*Rats! / They fought the dogs and killed the cats* . . .' We shout the lines at each other on our way home from lessons, in our bedroom, outside on the beach, on the windy cliffs: never in Mrs Oliver's hearing. (Smith 2009: 76)

Later, however, when their parents are alerted to Mrs Oliver's pedagogical limitations – as the girls' father puts it, 'it turns out she's a prize idiot – a nincompoop' – they acquire a new teacher. Much to their surprise, Miss Howard immediately 'fixes her full attention' on the children, as opposed to fawning over their parents:

> What . . . do we consider to be our favourite subjects? This is harder to answer. *Subjects* at Mrs Oliver's establishment were as good as non-existent. We glance at each other for inspiration.
> 'Books', we declare, simultaneously.
> 'Stories – and poems', my sister adds. Then, wishing to be more helpful, she enlarges her reply; 'Ellie likes writing things, and I like drawing – and painting pictures.'
> 'I see,' says Miss Howard, with a nod. And we have the impression that she does see. (Smith 2009: 198)

Miss Howard's approach to teaching and learning is a revelation to the sisters. 'Ever since Mrs Oliver was replaced as our instructress by Miss Howard we can't be sure, Pam and I, from morning to morning, what may be going to happen next' (Smith 2008: 218). One day another child brings an enormous jellyfish to school, having found it stranded on the beach after a storm:

> Miss Howard, peering into the bucket, as intrigued as we were, said that she thought it might possibly be a Portuguese Man o' War, which – apparently – is a species of jellyfish very seldom seen anywhere near the coast of Cornwall. She instructed Kathleen Keily to look it up in one of the several big red encyclopaedias kept on the topmost shelf of our schoolroom. And sure enough, Miss Howard, who knows such a lot about such a lot, was quite right. There, for proof, on a page of the great heavy volume, was a picture and the description of a Portuguese Man o' War: the Keilys' jellyfish. Instead of a geometry lesson, we were allowed to draw this rare visitor to our shores, and to colour our drawings, before the Keilys carried it back across the River Gannel and returned it to the sea off Crantock beach. (Smith 2009: 218)

On another occasion, they look up in the top-shelf encyclopaedia a rare and fascinating species of plant which happens to grow locally; Miss Howard then takes her pupils to see it. 'Never in a million years could we envisage going with Mrs Oliver on an expedition up to Bodmin Moor so as to search out and make drawings of an insect-eating sundew – *never!*' (Smith 2009: 219). Miss Howard might never have heard of VAKT, Gardner's MI profiling or Kolb's learning cycles, but she seems to have known well enough that children learn in different ways. In terms of curriculum design, it seems her aim was to organize lessons in such a way that all her students were able to work in ways they found congenial some of the time while also ensuring that they experimented with other types of task. Eighty-odd years later, Philip Beadle has questioned the personalized learning agenda which came to the forefront of the UK government's thinking in the latter half of the first decade of the new millennium. 'Assessing students' learning styles, keeping the data and using it to plan lessons is, like the rest of the cod-psychological tosh on the web, a bucketful of nonsense. You cannot take a snapshot of someone's preferences on one day and use it to plan their whole future, as their responses are dictated by mood. . . . The notion of personalised learning . . . worries me. No teacher in the world has the time or technical ability to plan a lesson that is differentiated thirty different ways. . . . Better to trust in teachers' experience and professional judgement about what their class requires' (Beadle 2006b: 3). It seems clear that the practical Miss Howard was adopting a much more pragmatic approach.

Moreover, even if it weren't palpably unworkable to accommodate the learning preferences of every student in the class, Vermunt suggests that what is needed is an element of 'constructive friction', where the teacher pushes students to become more autonomous learners, and Grasha argues that since learners need to be 'stretched', deliberately mismatching their preferred learning style and the method of teaching might well be appropriate (Vermunt 1998 and Grasha 1984 in Coffield et al. 2004a: 40). In practice, well-meaning attempts to assess pupils' personal learning styles (often heavily influenced by Gardner) have often been more summative than formative, although it is hard to see much point in establishing how anyone learns unless that information is then be used to develop their learning. If MI theory generates more wide-ranging, multidimensional and creative classroom teaching then it still earns its place in our pedagogical thinking, but it is more important to promote a metacognitive approach which helps students develop a flexible and creative repertoire of learning skills, as we saw Melanie begin to do earlier in this chapter. With no research evidence to show that matching teaching methods to individual learning styles is more effective than incorporating content-appropriate forms of presentation and response for all students, what we can say is that the most successful learners in the future will be those who can access and process information multimodally and have some awareness of their own learning preferences.

Making students aware of different ways of learning can help them develop their strengths and encourage them to try less favoured approaches, but they must feel in control of their learning and qualified to judge their own progress. Achieving a metacognitive awareness of not only her own learning choices but also the range of strategies being used by her peers could have helped Laura, whom we met earlier in this chapter, develop valuable interpersonal and intrapersonal skills, but this did not happen. As learning styles sceptic Steven A. Stahl points out, there are some learning activities which it seems clear almost everyone will benefit from regardless of their supposed learning preferences. He characterises some learning styles inventories, which consist of making forced choices from a range of statements, as more akin to fortune-telling than scientific research, arguing:

> the problem with choices like these is that people tend to make the same choices. Nearly everyone would prefer a demonstration in science class to an uninterrupted lecture. This does not mean that such individuals have a visual style, but that good science teaching involves demonstrations. Similarly, nearly everybody would agree that one learns more about playing tennis from playing than from watching someone else play. Again, this does not mean that people are tactile/kinesthetic, but that this is how one learns to play sports. (Stahl 1999: 3)

There are certain types of visual text, for instance, that the vast majority of learners understand almost instinctively, such as maps, timelines and pie charts. As teachers it can be very productive to tap into students' intuitive ability to mediate such texts by reformatting key information or, of course, enabling students to do this for themselves. Thus, for instance, a pie chart might illustrate the relative textual space occupied by the various narrators of a text such as *Wuthering Heights,* with a timeline to clarify the complex history of the Earnshaws and the Lintons.

With regard to the kinaesthetic dimension, Shirley Franklin suggests that 'the merits of activity-based learning, as proposed by Vygotsky and Piaget, benefit all pupils, not just the more dextrous and active ones.... [well-designed kinaesthetic tasks] should not be used to calm active pupils, or as a sop to the non-academic sporty ones, but positively as an aid to learning' (Franklin 2006: 84). Perhaps if the visual and kinaesthetic activities Laura was asked to tackle had been accompanied by other options she might have been able to visualize and connect the phases of her learning more effectively: when planning any lesson sequence it is vital to review the activities we intend to offer and assess how they fit into the bigger learning picture.

Learners vary in the type and level of support they need, their motives for learning, their long-term goals, prior experience, level of self-awareness and level of metacognition. At a whole-school level, metacognitive learning may take the form of a skills portfolio, whereas in the classroom each lesson (and each part of each lesson) needs to be assessed in terms of the knowledge, skills or experience to be gained. As we saw in Chapter 1 of this book when looking at the learning activities planned for Natalie and Mark, in process work, when the outcome is determined and assessed by the teacher, it is often possible to design tasks which allow pupils to learn in different ways and demonstrate their knowledge and skills in various ways too. Here, as well as actually being allowed to write about *The Lady of Shalott*, Laura might also have benefited from listening to a recording of her group's discussions. Able students who enjoy working independently and individually can find collaborative tasks very challenging, but as Vygotsky tells us, talking aids thinking. When students share their thoughts and ideas with other learners, Vygotsky believes:

> an *interpersonal process is transformed into an intrapersonal one.* Every function in the child's cultural development appears twice: first on the social level, and later, on the individual level; first *between* people (*interpsychological*), and then *inside* the child (*intrapsychological*). This applies to voluntary attention, to logical memory and to the formation of concepts. All the higher functions originate as actual relations between human individuals. (Vygotsky 1986 in Franklin 2006: 86)

It will be worth bearing this quotation in mind when we revisit Vygotsky in Chapter 4. In the long run, if we take care to view 'learning styles' as patterns of working rather than innate personality traits we can avoid the labelling trap and acknowledge that all students benefit from extending and developing their repertoire of communication strategies and ways of making meaning. In Vygotskian terms, because Laura was unable to develop interpsychologically she was necessarily unable to progress intrapsychologically either. In order to plan for the learning of all our students, therefore, we must design a range of appropriately differentiated activities which will enable them to learn and also reflect upon what they have learned, how they learned it and how they can reapply those skills in the future. We want the schools in which we work to value and reward a wide range of student potential through the curricula they offer, while encouraging students to persevere at those aspects of learning they find challenging, and we want to avoid the depressing conclusion that the capacity to learn is pretty much all down to birth, upbringing or social circumstances, so we might as well give up. When all is said and done, if the learning styles concept leads us towards a thoughtful holistic re-examination of assessment for learning, differentiation, equality of opportunity, metacognition and multimodal literacies, it retains its status as a valid and relevant pedagogical approach.

Thinking Skills

Chapter Outline

Key Questions

The following key questions underpin the chapter:

1. Bearing in mind David Almond's Michael (see the following) and Laura (Chapter 3) what kinds of thinking do we really encourage – or perhaps it would be more accurate to say permit – in schools?

2. Are the modes of discourse which are privileged and mediated within our educational system designed either to promote, or actually to 'normalize' – or even to discourage – thinking?

3. Are we able to recognize thinking when (or if) it happens in our classrooms?

4. What are the implications for our pedagogy and our management strategies if we truly commit ourselves to making our schools environments in which thinking can flourish?

5. Finally – and perhaps most disconcerting of all – are we prepared to live with the consequences of encouraging our students to think – really think?

Thinking skills: some questions and issues

There is a scene in David Almond's novel *Skellig* where the protagonist, Michael, shows his English teacher, Miss Clarts, a story he has written. In the story, a boy befriends an old, neglected tramp who happens to have angel's wings. The boy and his friend, Kara, nurse the tramp back to health and he, in turn, teaches the two children how to fly before eventually taking to the skies and disappearing. Miss Clarts is so moved by the power of Michael's narrative that she starts to cry.

Miss Clarts no doubt felt a sense of professional satisfaction as a result of this classroom exchange. What English teacher would not be moved when witnessing one of their students using language so powerfully and imaginatively? The problem is, Michael's story is actually true: *he* is the boy in the narrative, his friend Mina is Kara and the tramp is Skellig, the angel Michael discovered one day when exploring the garage of his new home. An interesting way into teaching Almond's novel is to ask students to imagine themselves in Michael's position: if they were to encounter an angel, who could they share the news with and – perhaps even more telling – what form of discourse might prove robust and credible enough to convey such a sensational, world-changing piece of information? Students struggle with this exercise, and for good reason. Michael is desperate to share the secret of his amazing discovery with his family and community, but the only way he can do this without being regarded as insane is to pretend that he is telling a story and that his piece of writing is a work of fiction inspired solely by his imagination. Mina is the only person with whom he can share his secret. It is not insignificant that she is home-educated and a reader of William Blake, a poet who, when a child, regularly claimed to see angels himself.

Skellig engages with some challenging philosophical positions regarding the nature of thought and perception, not least those posited by the eighteenth-century thinker, Immanuel Kant. In his *Critique of Pure Reason*, (1781) Kant argued that the human mind can only experience objects which exist within an empirical realm bounded by time and space: metaphysical concepts such as 'God' or 'the soul' – or 'angels', even – lie beyond 'real', empirical comprehension and can only therefore be considered in 'ideal' terms. By entering Michael's garage, Skellig crashes through the boundaries between the metaphysical and the empirical and thus forces a radical reconfiguration of the boy's thought processes. There is nobody at Michael's school to whom he can talk openly about this momentous experience – something so important that it amounts in effect to what the historian and philosopher Georges Canguilhem calls an 'epistemological break' (Macey 2001: 55) with past ways of knowing . Before resorting to writing fiction for Miss Clarts, Michael tries to broach the subject more directly by raising the biological possibility of human flight with his Science teacher. Again, he is met with the same kindly meant incomprehension.

Interestingly, David Almond's novel first appeared in 1998, a year in which the newly elected Labour Government of the United Kingdom initiated a major review of thinking skills in the classroom (McGuinness 1999). Since then, the government declares, 'interest in the teaching of thinking skills has burgeoned in the UK' to such an extent that there are now well over 60 different programmes in operation, a dedicated space is reserved for thinking skills on the government's *Standards* website (DfES 2010), and 'personal, learning and thinking skills' have been included in the statutory National Curriculum (QCDA 2010). Perhaps, if Almond were to write *Skellig* today, his protagonist Michael would find the school environment had changed so radically as a result of this sustained intervention that he felt able to share openly his thoughts about his ground-breaking discovery without fear of ridicule or worse. As it is, the actual reception of Michael's 'epistemological break' suggests that in 1998 a great deal of work needed to be done. Michael's Science teacher applauds his interest in the possibility of human flight – but dismisses his enquiries by saying that the class has already 'done' Evolution and needs to move on to other parts of the syllabus. Miss Clarts is moved to tears by Michael's story but – and perhaps her uncomprehending kindness makes the action all the more insidious – she actually gives him the covert message that his senses are not to be trusted and that there is no form of discourse available within her classroom which would allow him to speak the truth about Skellig. If Laura's experience, described in Chapter 3, of having to draw maps of Shalott when she would rather engage with the thematic and linguistic intricacies of Tennyson's complex poem are typical of today's classrooms, it seems as if we still have a long way to go.

This extract from Almond's novel should, therefore, give English teachers interested in thinking skills pause for thought. However, before we rush to embrace the idea, we would do well to recall the following cautionary words about the implementation of new educational initiatives. They come from the opening of a recent report into English teaching by a team from England's Office for Standards in Education (OFSTED):

> Where the curriculum was least effective, the teachers had found it difficult to respond creatively to the new opportunities. They were implementing national policy changes unthinkingly, often because they had no deeply held views about the nature of English as a subject and how it might be taught. (2009: 19)

Following OFSTED's advice, we need, before committing ourselves, to ask some uncomfortable questions. Finding honest answers to those questions requires us to undertake some difficult thinking of our own concerning – to quote OFSTED again – 'the nature of English as a subject and how it might be taught'.

We might begin to address these questions by establishing, first, why a concept which seems so obviously laudable in theory might actually be, in practice, a potential cause for concern. Take as an example those 'personal, learning and thinking skills' embedded in the statutory National Curriculum for England mentioned earlier. The qualities they are designed to promote are praiseworthy. Students are to become

- independent enquirers
- creative thinkers
- reflective learners
- team workers
- self-managers
- effective participants.

The National Curriculum documentation provides further information for each of the six areas in terms of what it calls *focus* and of the *skills, behaviours and personal qualities* characteristic of successful practitioners. Homing in on just one of the six as a further example, here is the *focus* statement associated with *team workers:*

> Young people work confidently with others, adapting to different contexts and taking responsibility for their own part. They listen to and take account of different views. They form collaborative relationships, resolving issues to reach agreed outcomes.

A set of bullet points describes their characteristic skills, behaviours and personal qualities. Effective team workers

- collaborate with others to work towards common goals
- reach agreements, managing discussions to achieve results
- adapt behaviour to suit different roles and situations, including leadership roles
- show fairness and consideration to others
- take responsibility, showing confidence in themselves and their contribution
- provide constructive support and feedback to others. (QCDA 2010)

Again, all of this sounds unexceptional – until we filter it through the lens provided by a radical social theorist such as Jürgen Habermas, 'one of the twentieth-century's leading philosophers whose work has inspired educationalists' (Morrison 2001: 221). Having gained his earliest experiences of teachers in Hitler's Germany, (Terry 1997) it would be understandable if Habermas were to cast an encounter like the one between Michael and his Science teacher (whose not entirely jocular nickname is *Rasputin*) in a sombre light. A Habermasian reading of the scene might interpret the total mismatch between the science that Michael wants and needs to think about and the science that *Rasputin* – the full weight of examination boards and syllabuses behind him – tells him he should think about, as a manifestation of *instrumental rationality*: a world view which has been defined as a series of 'interests, expressed through the medium of work', which 'focus on the material production necessary for our existence' (Ewert 1991: 348) to the detriment of aesthetic or moral concerns. 'From the instrumental perspective', Ewert continues, 'teaching becomes the management of standardized ends and means; learning becomes the consumption of prepackaged bits of information and parts of skills; and success becomes teachers and students doing as directed' (1991: 350). The description might have been written for *Rasputin's* dismissal of Michael's enquiry.

Now apply the same Habermasian reading to the National Curriculum's account of the personal, learning and thinking skills associated with effective *team workers* described earlier. Imagine a post-Fordist industrial situation in which a Japanese-style 'quality circle' of workers is building a car. It would be possible for the team to meet all the National Curriculum criteria by focussing exclusively, in an instrumentally rational way, upon the task of car making. One could 'show fairness and consideration to others', for example, by using language courteously in the workplace while constructing the car or by ensuring that the work-load was spread equitably among the group. What might look like a successful illustrative model in terms of National Curriculum criteria does not seem quite so attractive when matched against a different set of standards:

> technological production has structured consciousness to think in terms of *mechanisticity* (seeing the work process as tied to a machine process), *reproducibility* (no action in the work process is unique but must be reproducible), *measurability* (the individual's activities can be evaluated in quantifiable terms), *componentiality* (everything is analyzable into constituent components that are seen as interdependent), *problem solving inventiveness* (a tinkering attitude

towards areas of experience that can be dealt with in terms of technological solutions), and the *self-anonymization of the worker* (learning to divide the self into component parts, and to accept the human engineering process that organizes the self in terms of technological functions). (Bowers 1977: 36–7)

Our quality circle of car workers, so successful in National Curriculum terms, could also be said to meet all these less attractive criteria which Bowers identifies as characteristic of instrumental rationality in the industrialized workplace. For the purposes of this chapter, one section of the quotation is particularly pertinent. Bowers suggests that, from an instrumentally rationalist perspective, 'problem solving inventiveness' is reduced to nothing more than 'a tinkering attitude towards areas of experience that can be dealt with in terms of technological solutions'. The bleak consequence, Bullough and Goldstein observe, is the reduction of 'moral, aesthetic, educational and political issues to technical problems: why and what are reduced to how' (1984: 144). The point is that our car workers could meet the National Curriculum criteria for effective team working without having to address the really big questions about car production which a 'moral, aesthetic, educational and political' perspective would demand. Why are we still making cars that rely on fossil fuels? Why is the energy and investment devoted to car making not given over to developing alternative forms of public transport or to finding ways of feeding the hungry of the world? Why, as the planet overheats so dangerously, are we still producing cars on a globally industrial scale?

Reflection Activity 4.1

Where do you stand on the issue of thinking skills? Are they another fashionable fad, or do they lie at the core of our work as English teachers? Is the Habermasian critique described earlier far-fetched, or does it raise important ideological issues which we need to consider in the classroom? What is your role as teacher: to prepare students to take their place in the world as it is, or to help them to change that world? What do other teachers in your school think, particularly those responsible for the teaching of citizenship?

As John Dewey put it a century ago, high-quality thinking must always be

more or less troublesome because it involves overcoming the inertia that inclines one to accept suggestions at their face value; it involves willingness to endure a condition of mental unrest and disturbance. . . . To maintain the state of doubt and to carry on systematic and protracted inquiry – these are the essentials of thinking. (1910: 13)

If we are really going to commit ourselves to teaching thinking skills, then that commitment has to be whole-hearted and not something which is constrained within the bounds imposed by instrumental rationality. Thinking skills are *triarchic:* they include creativity and analysis as well as practicality – witness the power and complexity of Melanie's presentation in Chapter 3 (Sternberg 1985).

Why thinking skills matter

The UK Government's own Department for Education and Skills (DES as it was then known) has defined thinking as a 'cognitive activity triggered by challenging tasks and problems' (McGregor 2007: 2). The 'challenges' and the 'problems' have got to be real ones. Thinking has always been a dangerous activity – as Socrates, who is credited with establishing dialogic problem-solving as an educational method in the West (Kutnick and Rodgers 1994) can testify. He paid for his inquisitiveness with his life. Living is also a dangerous activity; but if our students are going to be able to negotiate it successfully, they must become – in the words of Maslow (1954) or Rogers (1983) – 'self actualized': able to think for themselves and to act autonomously. Key theorists have stressed the crucial importance of this educational goal. As Bruner puts it in a statement antithetical to the instrumental rationalist model of education: 'truths are the product of evidence, argument and construction rather than authority, textual or pedagogic' (1996: 57). For Vygotsky, this move towards autonomous learning is central to cognition:

> Vygotsky's theory of cognitive development rests heavily on the key concept of internalization. . . . The child first experiences active problem solving activities in the presence of others but gradually comes to perform these functions independently. The process of internalisation is gradual; first the adult or knowledgeable peer controls and guides the child's activity, but gradually the adult and child come to share the problem solving functions with the child taking the initiative and the adult correcting and guiding when she falters. Finally, the adult cedes control to the child and functions primarily as a supportive and sympathetic audience. (Brown and Ferrara 1985: 281)

Erik De Corte, too, sees the ceding of control from teacher to student – so that the latter can develop what he calls 'cognitive and volitional self-regulation' – as one of the main characteristics of powerful learning environments:

> environments that intend to foster the productive use of knowledge and skills should initiate active and constructive learning processes in students.

In language similar to that quoted from the DES earlier, De Corte continues:

> productive learning and the preparation for future learning can be fostered by
> confronting students as much as possible with challenging, realistic problems and
> situations that have personal meaning for them, and are representative for the
> kind of tasks they will encounter in the future. (2003: 25)

For Habermas himself, this ability to think autonomously, flexibly and resil-
iently is not only educationally desirable. He regards the capacity to participate
in 'rational discourses' (1996: 107) as essential if human beings are ever to find
peaceful, democratic and equitable solutions to the challenges they face:

> This discourse principle is the normative foundation of democracy in Habermas'
> sense. . . . If it is followed, each citizen can participate in public affairs on equal
> terms. Rationality here means that consensus must only be reached on the
> grounds of the better argument. Thus, it excludes every form of violence, threat,
> and external influence, that is it excludes the right of the stronger or the more
> powerful to prevail. (Carleheden 2006: 527)

Thinking skills and the English teacher

Teachers of English are particularly well placed to help their students to
think in the fullest sense of the word suggested here by De Corte, Dewey and
Habermas.

Reflection Activity 4.2

Do you think the above statement is true? If so, what opportunities does English teaching
afford for the development of thinking skills? What opportunities do other subject areas
provide – Maths or Physics, for example? How can we work with colleagues across the
curriculum divide (and beyond the school context) to encourage purposeful thinking in
our students?

The most obvious reason for asserting that English teachers are particularly well placed with regard to thinking skills is that our stock in trade is
language, expressed through the four modalities of speaking, listening,
reading and writing. As Fisher (2000) puts it, what makes the human mind so
powerful is

> the use of speech for learning, and in particular an elaborate syntax linked to a
> powerful symbolic memory which enables humans to elaborate, refine, connect,
> create and remember great numbers of new concepts. (McGregor 2007: 19)

The primary focus, therefore, for English teachers committed to developing their students' thinking skills must be the modalities of speaking and listening. In a direct challenge to his exact contemporary, Jean Piaget's, assertion that cognition starts with the individual and then moves outwards, Vygotsky argues that the 'primary function of speech, in both children and adults, is communication, social contact' (1986: 34). He continues:

> the true direction of the development of thinking is not from the individual to the social, but from the social to the individual. (1986: 36)

We learn by listening to, observing and imitating others. In addition, the pressure of having to articulate our thoughts and feelings for those who share what Habermas would call our 'lifeworld' helps us not only to refine our thinking but also to generate new thoughts and thus to nurture the sophisticated 'mindware' (Perkins 1995) of what Vygotsky calls 'inner speech'. If we follow Vygotsky's ideas here, then our classrooms have the potential to become powerful spaces in which thinking can flourish – but only if we create opportunities for purposeful speaking and listening.

The importance of purposeful talk

After years of relative neglect – in which they remained the poor relations of their more conventionally 'academic' (and therefore assessable) counterparts, reading and writing – the true cognitive power of speaking and listening is at last being recognized. In the context of the United Kingdom, particular credit for this must go to Robin Alexander for his sustained efforts to research and identify 'an "emerging pedagogy" of the spoken word' (2005: 1). Drawing upon two decades of international research, Alexander echoes Vygotsky by arguing:

> Language not only manifests thinking but also structures it, and speech shapes the higher mental processes necessary for so much of the learning which takes place, or ought to take place, in school.

He continues:

> It follows that one of the principal tasks of the teacher is to create interactive opportunities and encounters which directly and appropriately engineer such mediation. (2005: 2)

Although lip service (literally, perhaps) might be paid to speaking and listening (they have been a statutory part of the National Curriculum for

England, for example, since its inception 20 years ago) Alexander discovered that, in practice, classroom talk tended to fall into two distinct and equally dismal categories:

> as many UK and US researchers have constantly found, one kind of talk predominates: the so-called 'recitation script' of closed teacher questions, brief recall answers and minimal feedback which requires children to report someone else's thinking rather than to think for themselves.

The alternative seemed to be:

> An endless sequence of ostensibly open questions which stem from a desire to avoid overt didacticism, are unfocused and unchallenging, and are coupled with habitual and eventually phatic praise rather than meaningful feedback. (2005: 3)

Reflection Activity 4.3

Consider a lesson you have taught recently. Better still, arrange for someone to film a lesson you are about to teach. Make a note of the language exchanges which take place during the lesson. How often do you find yourself engaging in one or other of the negative uses of talk described previously by Alexander. (Be honest!) What measures could you take to prevent yourself from slipping into either of these two modes?

Like Miss Clart's and *Rasputin's* responses to David Almond's Michael, or the teacher's suggestion that Laura should focus in her textual engagement with *The Lady of Shalott* on a round of map drawing and freeze framing, both these approaches send out negative ideological messages to our students: either the classroom is a place where an adult does all the talking and they are meant to listen in almost total silence, or else – and perhaps this response, like Miss Clart's, is the more insidious because it is kindly intentioned – they are patronized and left bewildered and directionless. It is no surprise, given this situation, that students should start taking matters into their own hands by, for example, setting up self-help discussion groups on the Internet where, perceiving themselves to be denied access to real learning in the classroom, they attempt together to puzzle out their own responses to national examination questions. One could spend some time unpacking the layers of anger, low self-esteem and sense of betrayal behind the genial bluster in this message from one such student of English Literature:

> worship ya all!!! i come from a ghetto school so most of my classmates are C/B-graded so my teacher never bother to give out tips to get A/A*, not even how the essay should be structured out. so you have no **idea** how much this thread hath help'd me:o

Laura might understand the emotions behind this message.

The lessons from Vygotsky and, latterly, Alexander, appear at last to be receiving official endorsement in the United Kingdom where a *socioculturalist* teaching and learning agenda is being promulgated in English classrooms. McGregor identifies this position as post-Vygotskian in that it builds upon his key concepts of the *Zone of Proximal Development, Teacher Mediation* and *Scaffolding* by emphasizing learning as an enterprise involving 'guided participation' and 'apprenticeship' (2007: 48). Thus, a recent publication from the Department for Children, Schools and Families (DCSF) sets out the following key principles of student participation in effective classroom dialogue:

- Everyone is engaged with the dialogue
- Teacher talk does not dominate the dialogue
- Pattern of dialogue is 'basketball' rather than 'ping-pong'
- Dialogue is reciprocal, that is, pupils respond to and build on what others have said
- Pupil contributions are well-developed sentences or phrases
- Pupils are willing to take risks by sharing partial understanding
- Pupils are willing to challenge each other's ideas in a constructive way
- Pupils demonstrate higher levels of thinking
- Pupils reprocess their thinking as a result of dialogue

In terms of guided participation and apprenticeship, the following teaching strategies are suggested:

- Rich questions
- Big questions
- Higher-order thinking questions
- Questions linked to resources or tasks
- Discussion requiring application of learning from previous lessons or subjects
- Dialogue that requires independent thought and work. (DCSF 2009: 11)

> **Reflection Activity 4.4**
>
> In the next lesson you teach which focuses upon speaking and listening in the classroom, use the foregoing checklist to help you plan for purposeful talk. Arrange for a colleague to observe the lesson. Afterwards, review it together and see if you can provide evidence for each point on the checklist. Are there any areas which you feel you can address easily? Are there any areas which prove difficult for you and your students to access? Why might this be and what steps can you take to improve the situation?

Creating a thinking skills classroom

How might these principles be translated into classroom practice? The next section of the chapter takes a number of the previously mentioned key statements in turn and attempts to tease out the practical and pedagogical implications of applying them in an English lesson dedicated to the promotion of high-quality thinking. It would be useful here to think again here about the references to Bernstein and to Kress in Chapter 3.

Principle

- Everyone is engaged with the dialogue
- Teacher talk does not dominate the dialogue

The American social scientist, Roger Garlock Barker, has alerted us to the significance of what he calls *behaviour settings* in mediating and conditioning learning (1968). The idea came to him when travelling by rail across the vast heartlands of small-town America. He recalls:

> The . . . train south passed through many small towns. They fascinated me. To my laboratory-conditioned eyes they were activity cages walled in by miles of almost uninhabited space so that most of the behaviour of the towns' children occurred within the cage walls. (1980: 106)

Barker drew the conclusion that the behaviour of individuals is heavily influenced by what he calls the *extra-individual* behaviour of the landscape and community in which the individual lives.

Equally pertinent in this context is the American psychologist James Jerome Gibson's work on the concept of *affordance* (1977). Affordance invites us to think about an object's potential as a tool for *affording* or *not affording* particular actions and behaviours, in the way that a staircase, for example, might *afford* access to a room for an able-bodied person but not for someone with mobility difficulties. If these references to Barker and Gibson seem an oblique way to preface a commentary upon dialogue, we need to remember that, for powerful thinking and talking to take place in our classrooms, the behaviour settings and affordances must be right.

Reflection Activity 4.5

Review your classroom. What **affordances** does it provide to encourage learning? What kind of **behaviour setting** does it provide? Would you like to learn in such an environment? If not, what can you do to improve it?

First, we need to think about the appearance – if not of the *activity cage* represented by the whole school, than at least of the classroom. Edward De Bono's long-established concept (see, for example, 2000) of the *Six Thinking Hats* strategy, designed to replace confrontational argument with what he calls 'parallel thinking' as a means of problem-solving, has encouraged us to associate particular colours with habits of mind. Thus, the *Black Hat* might represent critical judgement, the *Green Hat* new ideas, the *Red Hat* emotions and so on. Could the classroom be painted in a series of colours, so that there might be a *Green* corner where exciting alternative ideas are explored? Or a *Yellow* corner, where participants are encouraged to think positively about a problem? And what kinds of images and texts are on the walls and around the room? We might have a digital photo frame or an interactive white board showing a series of images associated with the key concepts and themes explored in the English lesson. There might be a *word wall* modelling the use of powerful metacognitive words such as *therefore, however, on the other hand, consequently.* Hanging from the ceiling might be brightly decorated mobiles with evocative images or key words associated with literary criticism. On the students' desks might be laminated place mats or individualized packets containing vocabulary resources or ideas designed to encourage thinking.

Does the layout of the room *afford* or hinder access to thinking? Serried rows of desks facing a whiteboard and a lectern may connote transmission teaching and the passive reception of information. A table set at the front of the room can act as a barrier between teacher and learners. Move that table into the middle of the room so that everybody can sit around it and the *behaviour setting* is transformed. Instead of a transmission model of learning, in which the teacher might act as the 'gatekeeper' to the knowledge embedded in the text, the new setting signals a more democratic, Habermasian commitment to a shared endeavour in which everyone has an equal opportunity to participate – literally so, because teacher and students are seated at the same level and each person can make eye contact with all the other people around the table. Paying attention to behaviour settings in this way can help bring vividly to life important educational concepts which might otherwise seem vague and incomprehensible to students. When everyone is seated round the same table, the teacher might remind the students how the etymology of the word *companions* has its roots in the precious communal activity of 'breaking bread' together and move on from this to explore Vygotsky's account of situated learning – or, particularly pertinent for a lesson involving engagement with literature – Stanley Fish's investigation of literacy criticism as the enterprise of an 'interpretative community' (1980).

Principles

- Pattern of dialogue is 'basketball' rather than 'ping-pong'
- Dialogue is reciprocal; that is, pupils respond to and build on what others have said

If everyone is seated together at eye level, we have more chance of breaking the stranglehold of the 'recitation script'. The metaphors used by the DCSF to describe types of classroom dialogue are particularly pertinent here. The *basketball* image evokes ideas of a team passing questions, speculations, responses between them, possibly in a set of strategic moves 'choreographed' by the teacher – or possibly with unexpected and dramatic changes of direction as the 'thought ball' is suddenly thrown from one side of the 'court' to the other. The 'movement' can be vertical as well as horizontal. Just as a basketball can be steered by a player crouching low over the ground, so it can be hurled high into the air as a team strives – by asking and responding to 'big' and 'rich' questions – for the 'net'. Perhaps it is time to leave the metaphor alone, before we become embroiled in the details of *time outs* and *slam dunks;* but the point still holds good, not least through that evocation of dialogue as a series of choreographed 'thinking' moves. Consider this metaphor again when you analyse the long transcript in Chapter 5.

Planning for thinking

Principle

- Pupils demonstrate higher levels of thinking

If dialogic talk in the classroom is to avoid the charge of being 'unfocused and unchallenging', as Alexander puts it, it must be planned for and it should be mapped against a taxonomy of thinking. There are many taxonomies to choose from, as Mosley et al. have described in a comprehensive review conducted on behalf of the English Learning and Skills Research Centre (2004). One of the most widely known is that published by Bloom et al. in 1956. Less well known, perhaps, is the revised version which Anderson, Krathwohl and other members of the original team undertook some 45 years later (Anderson et al. 2001; see also Chapter 5). Surprised by the enthusiasm with which the 1956 taxonomy was received by educational practitioners and eager to update their work in the light of developments in cognitive psychology, the team introduced a number of significant changes. These included the addition of a fourth, *metacognitive*, knowledge dimension; the recasting of their six 'cognitive processes' as active verbs; the introduction of *remember* and *understand* as part of these processes and, perhaps most tellingly, the replacement of the higher order process of *synthesis* with the verb *create*. 'One of the most frequent uses of the original Taxonomy', Krathwohl (2002) recalled, 'has been to classify curricular objectives and test items'. In a phrase reminiscent of Bowers' attack on instrumental rationality cited earlier, he criticized this approach, arguing that:

> Almost always, these analyses have shown a heavy emphasis on objectives requiring only recognition or recall of information, objectives that fall in the *Knowledge* category.

To focus on these areas, Krathwohl continued, is to miss the key pedagogic point, because:

> it is objectives that involve the understanding and use of knowledge, those that would be classified in the categories from *Comprehension* to *Synthesis*, that are usually considered the most important goals of education. (2002: 213)

In the revised taxonomy, the four knowledge dimensions are defined as follows:

> **Factual Knowledge** – The basic elements that students must know to be acquainted with a discipline or solve problems in it.
> **Conceptual Knowledge** – The interrelationships among the basic elements within a larger structure that enable them to function together.
> **Procedural Knowledge** – How to do something; methods of inquiry, and criteria for using skills, algorithms, techniques, and methods.
> **Metacognitive Knowledge** – Knowledge of cognition in general as well as awareness and knowledge of one's own cognition. (2002: 214)

The following checklist reproduced from Krathwohl (2002) plots these four knowledge dimensions against the six cognitive processes. It is a particularly valuable planning tool for our purposes because it can be applied to two key areas explored in this book. If we were concerned in this chapter with differentiation, for example, we could prepare a series of questions and tasks at each of the six levels of cognition, in an attempt to create textual *affordance* for students with a wide range of abilities. However, if, as in this chapter, thinking skills are our focus, we need to bear Krathwohl's point in mind and make sure that our work across all four knowledge dimensions is targeted at the higher end of the cognitive spectrum. Taking our cue from the revised taxonomy, we must be sure that the learning outcomes for our lessons contain those all important active verbs which signal the crucial principle that *learning*

Table 4.1

The knowledge dimension	1. Remember	2. Understand	3. Apply	4. Analyze	5. Evaluate	6. Create
A. *Factual Knowledge*						
B. *Conceptual Knowledge*						
C. *Procedural Knowledge*						
D. *Metacognitive Knowledge*						

lies at the heart of all we do in the classroom. Examples might include the following:

> Students will be able to apply . . .
> Students will develop their ability to analyse . . .

In order to apply these principles to an English classroom, imagine that a class of 16-year-old Literature students are studying the opening chapter of Charles Dickens' novel *A Christmas Carol* (1843). They have just read this famous description of the main character:

> Oh! But he was a tight-fisted hand at the grind-stone, Scrooge! a squeezing, wrenching, grasping, scraping, clutching, covetous, old sinner! Hard and sharp as flint, from which no steel had ever struck out generous fire; secret, and self-contained, and solitary as an oyster. The cold within him froze his old features, nipped his pointed nose, shrivelled his cheek, stiffened his gait; made his eyes red, his thin lips blue and spoke out shrewdly in his grating voice. A frosty rime was on his head, and on his eyebrows, and his wiry chin. He carried his own low temperature always about with him; he iced his office in the dogdays; and didn't thaw it one degree at Christmas.

How might we help the students access the higher cognitive processes while at the same time encouraging them to take responsibility for their learning? One interesting approach – developed from the creativity tests devised by the American psychologist Joy Paul Guildford (1967) – might be to invite them to bring to the next lesson an object which they feel expresses some key trait of Scrooge's character depicted here. It would be possible, of course, for the students to interpret the task in a literal manner and return with a piece of flint, perhaps, or an oyster shell. But what if we were to raise the cognitive stakes by saying that literal interpretations of the passage are not allowed? The teacher might model the task by showing the class a picture of a pregnant business woman hurrying to work at rush hour through the streets of London. The teacher might tell the students that this is her response to the image of the oyster. Or she might bring in a cheese grater and a piece of cheese, saying that the former represents Scrooge's voice and the latter represents language. The students' task is to question the teacher until they have worked out what the connections are. They can then replay the game with their own chosen objects. In terms of the four knowledge dimensions in the revised taxonomy, one can see how students would require *factual* knowledge about the story in order to engage with the task at all. Finding an object which illuminates a trait of Scrooge's character suggests that they have demonstrated *conceptual* knowledge. By modelling the activity for the students, the teacher has helped them to develop their *procedural* knowledge. As far as thinking skills are concerned, however, perhaps the most important of the four dimensions – the one which the team felt was lacking from the original version of the taxonomy – is *metacognitive* knowledge. It is vital in this context not only to give students a language to think with but also to help them understand and appreciate exactly how and why they deploy their favoured thinking strategies. Visual stimuli (see also Chapter 3) which draw upon Bruner's concept of *iconic representation* – such as concept and mind maps, Venn diagrams and 'learning trees' – can help students to organize and to track their thoughts.

Principles

- Pupils are willing to take risks by sharing partial understanding
- Pupils are willing to challenge each other's ideas in a constructive way

Figure 4.1

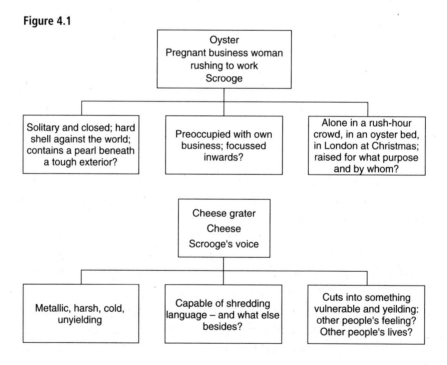

The more disparate the objects which require connection, the more opportunity there is to think imaginatively and – as the current English National Curriculum suggests – to take risks and to play with language. The proviso must be, of course, that the relationships between the objects can be supported with evidence from the text. By modelling the activity for the students first, the teacher not only demonstrates how the exercise works but also leads by example, showing the students that taking risks, thinking boldly and innovatively, are qualities to be welcomed in the classroom. As the students present their analogies, other members of the group can ask *sequenced* (rather than single) follow-up questions targeted against the higher spectrum of the taxonomy's *cognitive processes* to push the thinking further. If each student produces a concept map of the kind illustrated in Figure 4.2 (below), the class will have a formidable resource at its disposal for exploring Dickens' text. Lines of connection might be established between the different concept maps – are there patterns of similarity or do they differ widely? Can the various responses be grouped in different ways? This second wave of activities provides further opportunity for encouraging 'basketball' patterns of dialogue as well as for posing those 'big' and 'rich' questions which access the higher cognitive processes of *application, analysis, evaluation* and *creation*.

Principle

- Pupil contributions are well-developed sentences or phrases

Equipping students with *metacognitive knowledge* is essential to the creation of a powerful learning environment (DeCorte et al. 2003). In terms of metacognitive discourses which might apply specifically to *A Christmas Carol*, one might wish to introduce the students to the language of literary criticism in general, and of the novel genre in particular, as well as offering them access to vocabulary designed to help them locate Dickens within his historical, artistic, social and political milieu. Beyond this, however, lies a deeper imperative regarding the language of metacognition. If thinking skills are to be of real value to students, it is most important that they are *transferable*; the ability to *apply* (to draw upon the language of the revised taxonomy again) acquired knowledge and cognitive processes to a new situation is another key feature of powerful learning environments (De Corte et al. 2003). Vocabulary associated with Dickens' life and times – words like *debtor's prison* or *blacking warehouse*, for example – may or may not prove to be transferable to other 'lifeworld' situations which our students might encounter. The knowledge of and ability to apply correctly conditional verbs, however, is another matter entirely.

In a recent broadcast on a UK radio station, an adolescent member of a South London gang was talking about the bleak round of fear and violence which made up his daily experience of life. He ended each new grim description with the phrase: 'That's how it is' – as though he were locked into a cycle of despair from which there was no escape. Words like these bring painfully to mind the quotation from Jerome Bruner cited in Chapter 1:

> To be in the subjunctive mode is . . . to be trafficking in human possibilities rather than in settled certainties. (Bruner 1986: 26)

If that young man could complete his refrain by adding, 'but it might be different', it is possible that he could begin to imagine a better, life-changing alternative – those 'possible worlds' that Bruner writes about. Teaching students how to apply verbs like *could, should, might,* or phrases like *on the other hand, alternatively, however* or *consequently* to the life situations they encounter is one of the most valuable and potentially empowering tasks that a teacher of English can undertake. How might we scaffold this learning? If we return again to Guildford's association exercise applied to *A Christmas Carol,* we might invite our students to redesign their concept maps, charting, in sentences containing metacognitive words and phrases, the imaginative moves they made in their attempt to link an element of Scrooge's character with their chosen object.

Figure 4.2

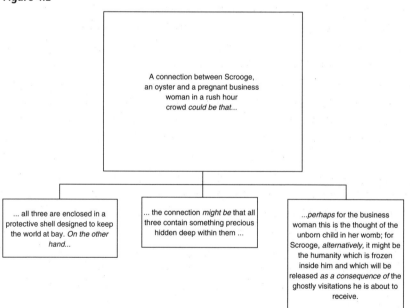

Scaffolded thinking strategies can be made more explicit through the use of *word stem* exercises which supply a basic frame within which students can experiment with language. The *rainbow poem* is one example. A variant of De Bono's suggestion that colours can be linked to elements of cognition, this exercise invites students to explore the symbolic potential of the colours of the rainbow while also, incidentally, reinforcing their understanding of the functions of the colon in a sentence and of the simile as a figurative device. Key words are supplied to a set pattern. Students have to fill in the gaps:

Scrooge's (students supply the emotion) *is* (students add a rainbow colour): (students repeat the colour) *as* (students complete the simile by drawing explicitly upon an image or theme suggested in Dickens' text):

> *Scrooge's* anger *is* red: red *as* the berry on a withered Christmas bough
> *Scrooge's* hope *is* orange: orange *as* the rising sun on the Christmas morning of his rebirth
> *Scrooge's* spite *is* yellow: yellow *as* the gold coins hoarded in his miser's chest

Thus, through the colour spectrum of the rainbow, each colour is linked to a particular emotion demonstrated by Scrooge during the course of the story. As before, the second, metacognitive element of the exercise requires the students to make explicit – either through their own prepared presentations or in response to 'rich' questioning from other members of the class – how rainbow colour, emotion and simile are linked by the text of *A Christmas Carol*. Almost by stealth, as it were, the students find that they have written a poem; again, with perhaps as many as 30 variations on this common theme within the class, the learning community has not only created for itself a powerful resource with which to explore further the intricacies of Dickens' story but also provided compelling evidence to support Vygotsky's assertion that we think and learn better when we actively engage upon a task with other people.

Literature as a resource

Principles

- Pupils are willing to take risks by sharing partial understanding
- Pupils demonstrate higher levels of thinking

These examples of how encounters with similes might encourage creative thinking in our students should remind us of what is perhaps the most significant reason why we as English teachers are particularly well placed to explore thinking skills. No other practitioners share our level of engagement with the tropes of figurative language which are the fundamental characteristic of literature. Think how a wealth of unspoken meaning can be concealed within an effective metaphorical conceit. In *Poem LIV* of A. E. Houseman's collection *A Shropshire Lad,* for example, the protagonist laments the untimely deaths of 'golden friends' – 'lightfoot boys' and 'rose-lipt maidens' – he once knew. The whole poem consists of only two verses, each four lines long. The horror of the loss is conveyed in the second verse:

> By brooks too broad for leaping
>   The lightfoot boys are laid:
> The rose-lipt girls are sleeping
>   In fields where roses fade.

How much suffering, how much concern for the human condition, lies unspoken behind those lines! How powerful, for example, is that image of the young men, so confident that nothing can break their stride (literally and figuratively). Approaching the brook, they see just another challenge which, overcome as easily as all the others in the past have been overcome, will serve simply to reassert their sense of invincibility. They leap into the air – and then realize, too late, that they will not reach the safety of the opposite bank. Houseman published *A Shropshire Lad* in 1896, almost 20 years before the Great War; but for this reader, at least, those lines evoke images of a lost generation going 'over the top' and perishing beneath a hail of machine-gun bullets in the Flanders mud. And this is another reason why powerful imagery is such a vital constituent of creative thinking. Houseman's image here resonates in the mind of the reader who then has to do the work for him or herself: making connections, teasing out the implications, responding with imagination, finding links with his or her own life.

Talk about metaphor and simile can be heard in most English classrooms – sometimes to dismal effect, as when students are invited to list the images they have found in a poem rather than to respond imaginatively, creatively and aesthetically to them. However, it is much less common to hear mention of their even more powerful cousins, the tropes of *synecdoche* and *metonymy*. If Houseman's brief, understated lines contain a wealth of implied meanings, consider the impact of this example of metonymy from Geoffrey Hill's poem *September Song*. The protagonist is addressing a young victim of the Holocaust. In language which is designed to mimic, with bitter irony, the inhuman detachment of the perpetrators of that crime, he describes the sequence of events which led to that horror as:

Just so much Zyklon and leather . . .

The sheer power of the compression here requires an even greater effort of the imagination – and, yes, given the nature of what is described – of the will on the part of the reader. The evil that the Nazis perpetrated is summed up as 'so much Zyklon and leather'. One sees the jackboots, the gleaming uniforms worn by those strutting criminals. One – what? smells? – the hydrogen cyanide produced industrially by the *German Corporation for Pest Control* [sic]. 'Smells' is hardly the appropriate word for so many reasons, not least because the Nazis ordered the removal of the statutory warning odorant which should have been included in the gas as a safety device. We said at the start of the chapter that, if we are really committed to thinking in the classroom, we must be prepared to live with the consequences of that thinking. As students and teachers for whom a key element of our work involves a sustained engagement with literature, we are used to being transported by the creative imagination into difficult places, and we are, by the nature of our calling, receptive to the challenge which real, concentrated thinking poses to us.

Using assessment to plan for thinking

Principle

- Pupils demonstrate higher levels of thinking

Bearing these points in mind, let us return to the Dickens' extract. One of the questions posed at the start of the chapter was: *Are we able to recognize thinking when (or if) it happens in our classrooms?* A key principle of this book is that effective planning and teaching for learning must be predicated upon detailed, focussed assessment. Let us imagine now that the student who produced the concept map linking Scrooge, the oyster and the pregnant woman has been asked to work that initial statement into a first draft of a more sustained, formal written response to the opening of *A Christmas Carol*:

> A connection between Scrooge, an oyster and a pregnant business woman in a rush-hour crowd could be that all three are enclosed in a protective shell designed to keep the world at bay. On the other hand, the connection might be that all three contain something precious hidden deep within them perhaps for the business woman this is the thought of the unborn child in her womb; for Scrooge, alternatively, it might be the humanity which is frozen inside him and which will be released as a consequence of the ghostly visitations he is about to receive.

Table 4.2

The knowledge dimension	1. Remember	2. Understand	3. Apply
A. Factual Knowledge	Scrooge receives a number of ghostly visitors on Christmas Eve	The messages brought by these visitors cause him to change his behaviour	How might our knowledge of Scrooge's character and our knowledge about the qualities of an oyster help us to perceive similarities between the two in the context of this impending change?
B. Conceptual Knowledge	Similes and metaphors can illuminate similarities and differences between seemingly disparate objects	Dickens' introduction into the text of words like *oyster, flint or grind stone* is an example of his craft as a writer. We need to honour that craft by reading beneath the surface of the text with alert attention so that we can really hear what he is trying to tell us	An effective simile will resonate on several levels of meaning. How many connections can we make between Dickens' description of Scrooge and the qualities of an oyster?
C. Procedural Knowledge	To engage with a text, one needs to apply both lower and higher order reading skills. When that text is a highly wrought, canonical work of fiction written almost 170 years ago, we need to draw upon our knowledge of other, similar texts we have read as well as upon our contextual knowledge of the period in which the story is set	We need to understand some basic principles of literary engagement. For example: whose voice speaks this text? What is the relationship between author, narrator and audience? How was this text received at the time of publication and how is it received today? Within what genre conventions does this text operate and how does this influence our reception of the text?	We need to apply our understanding of how and why novel writers in general (and of this period specifically) tell their stories in the ways that they do. Thinking of A Christmas Carol in particular, we might bring to the text our knowledge of Dickens and his times; our understanding of the conventions of allegory; the significance of Christmas within Christian culture.
D. Metacognitive Knowledge	We need to remember our own reading histories, preferences and qualities. What strategies for working with (or even against) the text do we possess for making meanings?	We need to understand the strategies that writers in general (and writers of C19 allegorical fiction in particular) might deploy in their texts. We need to know that readers produce pluralities of readings and that these readings might be influenced by a number of variables such as class, age, gender, race and experience	Focussing for an example upon the extract from the novel cited above, we need to be alert to the patterns running through the text and to be aware of the influence the deployment of this rhetoric is trying to exert upon us: the sequence of present participles; the use of alliteration and assonance; the inclusion of three exclamation marks; the way the paragraph starts – like the opening of Beowulf – with an ejaculation; the images of cold which are threaded through the writing

Thinking creatively ourselves about the chart derived from Krathwohl et al.'s revision of Bloom's Taxonomy, we could consider it in terms of two metaphors: a map and a scaffold. In the following worked example (Table 4.2 above), the contents of the student's response have been mapped against the four *knowledge dimensions* and the first (albeit lowest) three of the six *cognitive processes*. The mapping function of the chart, building upon Vygotsky's concept of the *Zone of Proximal Development*, enables us to see not only what the student can and cannot do but also to identify potential areas to which this exercise has not yet afforded access and thus not afforded opportunities to demonstrate ability.

Configured in terms of a scaffold, the chart can help teacher and student prepare a more focussed engagement with the set task. The stimulus material introduced at the start of the lesson by the teacher – the picture of the pregnant business woman hurrying to work in a rush-hour crowd – has served its scaffolding purpose by helping the student tease out the metaphorical connections between Dickens' portrayal of Scrooge and his use of the *oyster* simile. Now that the connection has been made, it can be discarded, just as a booster rocket might fall away from a space vehicle, once it has performed its task of breaking through the gravitational field of the earth's atmosphere.

Reflection Activity 4.6

Now it is your turn. Having modelled the activity, it is now time – to follow a second precept of Erik De Corte – for 'teacher fade'. You have a choice of two, differentiated tasks.
You can

Complete the mapping and scaffolding exercise for the Dickens' extract, filling in the knowledge dimension boxes for the three remaining higher order cognitive processes: **analyse, evaluate and create.**
Then: choose an assignment task from a literature syllabus of your choice and design a question which could be applied to A Christmas Carol.
Then: use the information derived from the completed chart to: (a) help you develop your sense of this student's Zone of Proximal Development with regard to the three higher cognitive processes, and (b) plan a sequence of learning activities which will help the student develop their thinking skills against the **four knowledge dimensions** and the **three cognitive processes** through their engagement with A Christmas Carol.

(*Continued on p. 106*)

Reflection Activity 4.6—Cont'd

Case study: Sally responds to *Skellig*

Alternatively, you might wish to attempt a similar exercise without the modelled example to help you and with a fresh text. Ending where we began, here is a student's blog response to a reading of the extract from David Almond's **Skellig** which introduced the chapter.

Your task is to track this student's statements against the taxonomy chart, completing all **four knowledge dimensions** and all **six cognitive processes**.

Then: as for parts two and three of the first exercise, you complete the instructions, substituting *Skellig* for *A Christmas Carol*.

The blog is reproduced as it was written:

> I found this session very enjoyable as Skellig is a very original book which, at first look would seem that it has very few links to educational ideas and the concepts we have considered in class, but once you delve into the different meanings and philosophies in the book you see that there are many ideas about schooling, imagination and conformity to name a few.
>
> One of the main themes I found interesting was the ideas about the school environment. In *Skellig,* the school is portrayed as repressive and making the children conform to only let them think about certain topics which restricted their education. This is shown when Michael talks to his teacher about the archaeopteryx, which relates to the topic they have been studying at school. However, this is the mythological side to evolution as it refers to 'Humans that are turning into creatures that can fly'. The teacher appreciates Michael's wider reading but tells him they are 'past evolution now' and goes on to talk about the biology of the body. I feel this is symbolic as the teacher is trying to repress Michael's imaginative and inquisitive thoughts and makes him learn information both that is definite as it is science, and that fits the strict academic criteria. It is interesting to consider that this book was written in a time when education was very much structured by the aim to pass exams. In the same extract, the teacher talks about the heart, 'our engine' purely in a physiological sense, which contrasts to Michaels inner thoughts that 'I could feel two hearts beating: the baby's and my own'. This shows that Michael is an emotive character, shown later in his expressive writing skills and his nurturing of Skellig, and the way the school is shaping him to not be expressive and are socializing him into the normative male role. Despite Michael later expressing himself in the way deemed appropriate for a male, 'The was blood trickling from a little cut around my eye' which I interpreted as a further use of the metaphor of the heart and blood (a symbol of his link to his sister) coming from his eye like a tear, showing, that he is still feeling sorrow about her illness.
>
> In contrast to this, Mina who Michael befriends is home-schooled and she is confident, creative and imaginative. I think this was David Almonds

way of commenting on repression of ordinary schooling. I agree that schooling makes us conform which can be repressive and the ability of to think freely and not be looked down upon for different practises or ideas lets us leave more progressive and creative lives. A. S Neill [a 'progressive' educationalist of the twentieth century] would agree with the ideas that David Almond puts across, as he believed that 'most unhappiness us due to inner hostility created in the child by external repression. However, I believe that shared education and therefore shared knowledge, values and ideals give people a common ground which can be a very positive thing for social cohesion. Equally, I believe that children need to be guided as with only free will, children may well lack structure which can mean a lack of security which can lead them to commit destructive behaviour both to themselves and to others. This links with Frankenstein as the monster is left to its own free will and is then labelled and isolated from society. I believe that schooling does not prepare us emotionally for life. I believe that emotion should not be separated from the school and the home, as teachers are guardians for children and should be there to prepare them for the wider world and therefore, it seems neglectful to not acknowledge the emotional and spiritual side to children's development.

5 Assessment

Key Questions

The five key questions which underpin this chapter can be summarized as the
who, what, when, where and how of assessment:

1. Who assesses and who is assessed? If assessment is to be more than
   merely something done to students by teachers, how can we help them
   to become confident and accurate assessors of their own learning? How
   can we contextualize the assessment information we have about our
   students to give external groups with a vested interest in knowing what
   our students can and cannot do (parents, employers, the government,
   further and higher education establishments) the fullest possible picture?

2. What does assessment tell teachers and pupils? Building on our work in
   Chapter 1, how do we ensure that assessment does more than reinforce
   what we, as teachers, and, crucially, our pupils already know – that is,
   that able pupils tend to do 'well' in tests and less able pupils tend to do
   'badly'?

3. When is assessment appropriate? How do we manage an assessment
   system in which high-stakes terminal testing remains the dominant
   method of quantifying and validating the diverse personal learning jour-
   neys of our students? Do we assess our new students at the beginning
   of the school year in order to find out about them, or at the end, to
   measure what we have taught them?

4. Where should assessment take place? If the classroom is a more appropriate context for assessment than the exam hall, how can we use this
   knowledge to plan for learning?

$\Rightarrow$

5. How can assessment aid teaching and learning? How can we encourage creativity, autonomy and independence as we prepare our students for crucial examinations as well as the wider world?

Assessment

Assessment means finding out what our students know or don't know and planning future work to meet their individual learning needs. It sounds so simple, yet powerful tensions have emerged over the past decade or so between the key notions of formative and summative assessment, and their implications for teaching and learning. Marking students' written work seems the most obvious way of assessing their progress, but this chapter will look at the pedagogical implications of using a model of assessment which uses oral rather than written evidence.

Case Study: Senior students studying Shakespeare

The pedagogical context for this chapter is the teaching of literature to older students. Seventeen-year-olds Rachel, Orla, Lucy and Heather have recently begun studying Shakespeare's *The Winter's Tale* for their UK A-level examination. As with the senior students discussing Thomas Hardy's poem *When I Set Out for Lyonnesse* in Chapter 1 of this book, it is worth noting that this is a small, single-sex group; moreover, as this lesson took place towards the end of their first year of A-level study, they already knew each other well and were very used to working together. It is also worth noting that the classroom layout here was carefully designed to afford equal access to all participants in the discussion, as teacher and students were seated around a circular table in the centre of the teaching space.

The students had been asked to read the first three scenes of Act IV of *The Winter's Tale* independently before the lesson during which the following assessment activity took place. At this point, the character of Autolycus the pedlar appears for the first time. At the start of the assessment activity, the students were given the following questions in order to guide their thinking and allow for an appraisal of their individual levels of understanding:

- What do you already know about the character of Autolycus?
- What do you still need or want to know about him?

Later in the lesson they were given some previously unseen contextual material, Louis MacNeice's poem *Autolycus*, and asked to re-evaluate their knowledge of

Case Study—Cont'd

The Winter's Tale using this new information. The question prompts at this point were:

- What happens if you compare Shakespeare's presentation of Autolycus with that of Louis MacNeice in this poem?
- How does MacNeice's poem fit with what we already know about this character and this play?

Here is a transcript of the students' responses to the first question.

Teacher: OK. So what do we know about Autolycus so far then?

Orla: He's a thief, isn't he? He steals from the Clown, the Shepherd's son. He's different from the people in Bohemia because they're quite trusting and noble whereas he's not.

Rachel: Well he opens Act Four Scene 3 with a speech in verse, singing, and so I think you automatically think this is light relief after all the killings and the massacre that's just occurred in the past and you think here's a slightly more comedic character.

Teacher: So what's he singing about?

Rachel: About the coming of the spring.

Heather: The seasons, which reflects the lighter spirit of the second half.

Rachel: Time's past . . .

Heather: . . . in Bohemia and not only Perdita, but spring will come back for Leontes.

Teacher: So you've got a new beginning and you've got a new type of character. What do you think Shakespeare's playing at here then? Why is there this sudden change, or is there continuity? Is there anything that would link us to what's gone before?

Rachel: I think he's saying that after winter there always will be a spring and Autolycus is a juxtaposition between the more royal, regal start – he's more of a countryman.

Heather: He's almost like you'd imagine a court jester.

Reflection Activity 5.1

Review the foregoing transcript of the students' first responses to MacNeice's *Autolycus*. What might this limited evidence tell us about the different patterns of ability, need and interest which exist here? You may wish to refer back to Chapter 4 here and use Anderson and Krathwohl's revision of Bloom's taxonomy to classify their learning and/or remind yourself of the material on differentiation which featured in Chapter 1.

Assessing the students' performance: Stage 1

As the first to speak, Orla confidently identifies Autolycus' role and compares his behaviour to that of the other Bohemians; 'He's a thief, isn't he? He steals from the Clown, the Shepherd's son. He's different from the people in Bohemia because they're quite trusting and noble whereas he's not.' Using Anderson and Krathwohl's remodelled version of Benjamin Bloom's original taxonomy of learning, Orla is going beyond *recalling* or *retrieving* previous information to construct meaning through *exemplifying* and *comparing*, which shows her textual knowledge is secure. It would be useful, however, to facilitate Orla's exploration of the text at a deeper and more challenging level so she can access the higher-order thinking skills identified by Anderson and Krathwohl, such as *analysing* and *evaluating*. In noting Autolycus' impact upon the structural 'break' in *The Winter's Tale* which differentiates the tragedy of wintry Sicilia and the comedy of fertile Bohemia, Rachel demonstrates a high level of conceptual awareness, which means she is already *analysing* and *evaluating* the text; Heather, too, in extending and developing Rachel's point, is creating relatively more complex textual readings than Orla – though the discussion is still at a very early stage.

As the only student who has not contributed to the discussion so far, there is as yet no way of assessing how far Lucy has made meanings of her own from the text; at present there is no evidence of even *remembering* – the most basic entry-level stage of Anderson and Krathwohl's taxonomy. Given Lucy's potentially fragile view of herself as a learner at this point, it is useful to think about Sadler's concept of 'guild knowledge', in which teachers transfer their own professional judgement about what being good at something means into their marking, so that the final grade given reflects how closely the work demonstrates the success criteria for that specific task (Sadler 1989 in Black et al. 2007: 2). Through effective formative assessment in the shape of feedback from her teacher and her peers, Lucy must be given permission (or give herself permission) to enter this particular 'guild', but to do so she needs to be shown what 'being good at English' looks like in this context.

In terms of Vygotsky's ZPD, it is clear that in many cases this crucial concept is subject to a high level of pedagogical control; as Knud Illeris has pointed out, in 'applying Vygotsky's learning concepts, teaching easily becomes a predominantly teacher-directed form of encounter which, in turn, can easily result in the nearest zone of proximal development being conceived of in the perspective of academic systematism, e.g. the next chapter in the textbook' (Illeris 2007: 59). Illeris goes on to endorse the redefined ZPD (or 'Zo-ped' as they call it) of Griffin and Cole, who argue that '[a]dult wisdom does not provide teleology for child development. Social organization and leading activities provide a gap within which the child can develop novel creative analyses.' They characterize this learning space attractively as 'a dialogue between the child and his future; it is a not a dialogue between the child and the adult's past' (Griffin and Cole 1984 in Illeris 2007: 60).

Valid formative assessment must enable Lucy to analyse and manage her own learning needs as far as possible although the teacher plays a crucial role in shaping the student's own view of her learning. The aim, as we saw during the discussion of 'affordances' in Chapter 4, is to facilitate a safe and welcoming classroom space in which experimental ideas are not allowed to fail; but while it is impossible to 'script' interventions which must be impromptu during an organic, ongoing and interactive classroom discussion, we need to think carefully about how targeted and differentiated questions can be used to assess students' individual current learning needs in order to help them make further progress. And of course, as in the student activity which underpins this chapter, questioning is a teaching method in its own right as much as it is a means of checking that learning has taken place.

Reflection Activity 5.2

Review the following transcript, which followed the students' individual silent reading of Louis MacNeice's poem *Autolycus*. What techniques are used by the teacher to facilitate the classroom discussion? How might these be adapted in your own practice? You might wish to refer back to the section in Chapter 4 of this book on the importance of managing purposeful classroom talk here.

Teacher: OK, so can we think about perhaps linking the poem and the play now?

Heather: The last line seems to sum up what he's saying throughout the poem, where it says, 'you too were born and grew up in a fix' – it's like the character of Perdita – it doesn't really matter that she was born and grew up in a fix; it's the end result, how she turns out, which matters.

Teacher: So you read that as a reference to Perdita there as well. So who's MacNeice talking to? Autolycus?

Orla: I don't think he was. He talks about the – where is it – the 'rogue that comes around the corner'.

Lucy: Oh yes . . .

Heather: And he also talks about 'the dramatist' and 'the master', and it's almost as if not only is that Leontes but it's also Autolycus because it's talking about how he's also dramatic and the master.

Rachel: Yes, I thought he was talking about Shakespeare predominantly in the poem and he also takes a step back and looks at the play as, well, it's this kind of jumble of 'tapestried romance' – and using 'tapestried' makes it sound rich and varied and quite, well, of Shakespeare's age. 'Classical bric-a-brac' . . . 'grottos' – he says this is something Shakespeare put together like a hotchpotch.

Teacher: And tapestries are made, aren't they? They're not accidental – someone has to weave them.

Heather: And it seems to be commenting on the play as a whole and maybe it's trying to insinuate that Autolycus is the one that's going to comment on the play and that maybe the poem is Autolycus's thoughts and things.

Teacher: I want to go back to what you said, though, Lucy . . .

Lucy: Oh no!

Teacher: Because you're right! You thought he was talking to Autolycus, and I think in that last verse, he is.

Lucy: OK . . .

Teacher: Because the rest of it, before that, like everyone says, it's more general, but that last . . .

Lucy: Yes, it's 'master pedlar with your tricks . . .'

Teacher: Yes, yes, and I really like that idea that at the end he says we all are born and grow up in a fix. What do you think he means there, Lucy?

Lucy: Oh no. I actually don't know! Can you come back to me in five minutes?

Teacher: Oh go on . . .

Lucy: It's kind of like he's summarizing it – it's coming back on to the actual character . . .

Heather: So it's almost as if he's referring to everyone else as a whole and moves on from talking about Autolycus to talking to him.

Teacher: You're both on to something! What's this idea about being 'born in a fix'? And I don't have an answer here. There's not an agenda here!

Lucy: Oh, so maybe he had a really nasty life.

Teacher: Maybe that's it. There's something about, look, what did people in Shakespeare's day do who were poor, who weren't necessarily born into power and authority, who basically had to find their own way . . .

Lucy: It's kind of universal – like Autolycus.

Teacher: In what way? How is it universal?

Lucy: Well, he's for all the poor people out there, do you know what I mean?

Teacher: And the idea that 'you too were born and grew up in a fix' – that for ordinary people life is challenging, difficult. MacNeice seems to be saying – well, what do you think his attitude to Autolycus reflects?

Lucy: He's sympathizing but not patronizing.

Rachel: Because he's come through it – as the characters will in the play.

Teacher: So do you think there's any significance about when this poem was written? The 1940s?

Lucy: Was it post-war?

Teacher: I think it probably was just after, but really even if it was during, the implication is . . . well, how does that link in with the rest of the play, do you think?

Lucy: Kind of 'we'll get through this.'

Orla: From 'taut plots and complex characters' – well that's like a war, isn't it?

Lucy: Yes – like Hitler.

Teacher: And who's in control of this play? Because some of you have mentioned Leontes, and some of you mentioned Shakespeare, and I suppose both of them are kind of really huge dominant characters aren't they? In control. So why does he refocus the play on Autolycus then? What's the point here?

Lucy: Because he doesn't really have control.

Heather: He doesn't really have power, as in he's not a king or anything. He only has power over the people he meets.

Lucy: He's got power in his own character not his role.

Teacher: So if we compare Shakespeare's presentation of Autolycus with MacNeice's, how do you think things have moved on?

Lucy: I think MacNeice's taking him more seriously.

Teacher: Why would he do that?

Rachel: Because Autolycus – he's stood the test of time – showing that this is a very universal thing that can be applied to any age.

Teacher: And what do you think about changing attitudes to the poor?

Lucy: They have changed.

Heather: Well, in Shakespeare's time it was considered your fault if you were poor. Like in the grand chain of being or whatever, that we did in History, where you were born is where you were supposed to be, whereas when MacNeice was writing it was considered to be unlucky – it wasn't as if it was your fault. It could just be circumstance and that there were no opportunities for you.

Teacher: So with Autolycus – well, we're told he's a thief. . . .

Lucy: It's like it's not, oh it's really bad that you're a thief, it's sympathy that you have to do that to survive.

Teacher: Yes, and in Shakespeare's day – well, has anyone heard of the Elizabethan Poor Law? Sounds like you might have done this period in History.

Lucy:	Yes, we did it in lessons Orla!
Teacher:	Well, they basically categorized people into two types – the deserving poor and the undeserving poor, saying these people deserve some charitable support – orphans, widows, the sick – but others . . .
Lucy:	Thieves, prostitutes . . .
Teacher:	Vagabonds . . .
Lucy:	Ruined maids . . .
Teacher:	Yes – and it's grouping people together and making it easier to stigmatize them by saying well, actually they've brought it on themselves. And MacNeice is challenging that, I think. So any lines that really made you think what he was playing at overall here?
Rachel:	'The stock-type virgin dance like corn in a wind . . . ' I think he's saying that those characters in Shakespeare's plays always crop up and he might be mocking it, saying they're clichés, but maybe he doesn't think that's a negative thing – that they are realistic.
Teacher:	And that first line 'in his last phase when hardly bothering to be a drama-tist' – well, is that a criticism?
Lucy:	I don't think it is. He didn't even bother, yet made this incredible character.
Heather:	It's as if he's going past the drama to almost the truth and commenting on morality.
Lucy:	Yes, it's less of a play rather than actual real life.
Heather:	Ideas tumble out just the same. It's more of a modern play than a traditional tragedy.
Teacher:	Something about form, then? 'Taut plots and complex characters to tapestried romances' is what MacNeice says.
Orla:	Sort of like in the future, isn't it? Not like all those period dramas.
Rachel:	'Sighting his matter through a timeless prism'.
Teacher:	So some things in this text escape the time in which they're set and start to make bigger points . . . and what about – well, MacNeice actually comes out with that word 'anachronism' – does everyone remember what that means?
Rachel/Heather/Orla:	Yeah . . .
Lucy:	Out of time.
Teacher:	So in a way it's a technical flaw or mistake . . .
Lucy:	But it doesn't matter.
Teacher:	MacNeice actually phrases it as 'None should want colour for lack of an anachronism.' He's almost suggesting it makes it more interesting.
Lucy:	Yeah, it does. Shakespeare didn't make mistakes! I think he was too good for that!
Teacher:	MacNeice mentions 'between acts three and four' – well we know what happens there, don't we – it's Time coming on – 'there was something

⇨

born which made the stock-type virgin dance like corn in a wind that having known foul marshes, barren steeps, felt therefore kindly towards Marinas, Perditas. . . . Thus crystal learned to talk.' What does that mean? I'd love to know what that means! What was crystal before it learned to talk?

Lucy: Stone?

Orla: It was beautiful, but it was silent . . . sort of . . .

Lucy: Oh! It could be the baby! It's hard at first isn't it, working it out – like the Brontë poems.

Teacher: You're on to something there. Maybe it's that Perdita, well although 'stock-type characters' were beautiful, they lacked a level of interest, whereas something happens with this late play, so characters become more interesting than what he calls those other stock-type virgins. Maybe 'Marinas and Perditas' are more interesting than other similar characters earlier on in his work?

Heather: So though Juliet was quite a forceful character in *Romeo and Juliet*, he could be almost commenting on the fact that she's being forced – her story's being played out and she's playing out a story that's been written for her, whereas Perdita's kind of driving her own story, and although they were both beautiful, it's the difference between feminist views of them.

Lucy: Yes, Perdita has gumption!

Teacher: Hey, maybe because she gets taken out of the royal court she's free to be acting out her own story? There's something else for us to think about next time.

Making meanings: reader-response theory and the assessment of students' approaches to literature

As Richard Andrews points out:

> The privileging of the reader in the act of reading is a humanist, teacherly position to take. It enables the exploration of a number of approaches to the reading of a text and due recognition of the role that readers play in the creation of meaning. Most significantly, emphasis upon the reader allows for pedagogical intervention in that it opens up the possibility of multiple meanings mediated by readers.

The business of teaching a book becomes not so much a matter of exegesis or leading one's students to 'appreciate' the qualities of a work, but enabling access to it and allowing the readers to make their own versions of it. (2001: 81)

While acknowledging that reader-response approaches to the teaching of literature have been accused of allowing 'disproportionate space to readers' so that 'they miss the subtleties embodied in the text,' Andrews is certainly right to suggest that such superficial readings 'are not so much a problem of the approach itself, but rather of a poor application of the approach' (Andrews 2001). While we must monitor the nature and quality of the interface between the individual reader and the text we should also acknowledge – and celebrate – the fact that the reading experience is immeasurably enriched by 'thinking about, or talking about, or writing about the work' (Squire 1990 in Andrews 2000). Reader-response theories are based upon the belief that writers and readers collaborate to make textual meanings and that the reactions of individual readers will depend upon their own experiences, ideas and values. If Rachel, Heather, Orla and Lucy understand this, they are set fair to think more analytically about other interpretations, critical positions and methods which they might use to examine distinctive aspects of a literary text or reconsider the same episode in a variety of ways.

West proposes that we take 'a more investigative and analytical approach to the whole question of literature' and go beyond 'endless sterile contention' about the nature and composition of literary canons, arguing that 'students must be free to make their own cultural and literary affiliations; our responsibility is to help them to a greater understanding of the implications of their own and others' choices. They need opportunities to see texts in their full social contexts and histories, to understand the assumptions underlying both the texts and the valuations put on them by particular groups' (Andrews 2001: 85). By resisting notions of teacher hegemony and fixed textual meanings, therefore, we can make space for a collaborative reciprocal discourse which not only models the 'basketball' dialogue patterns outlined in the previous chapter of this book but actively revels in the shifting and unstable nature of the text itself.

Benton and others draw attention to the fact that 'in the interaction between reader and text, the reader attends twice, to the world of the text, and to the world within him, generated by the text' (Andrews 2001: 87). As the students read MacNeice's *Autolycus* they enrich and deepen their understanding both as individuals and as a collective. As Andrews suggests, reading 'becomes a wave-like activity, with successive readings washing over the text, each wave bringing more to the reading and carrying the residue not only of previous experience ("real" and literary) but of earlier readings' (Andrews 2000). Here *Autolycus* meshes so suggestively with the students' previous reading of *The Winter's Tale* that MacNeice himself becomes not so much a great writer but also – crucially – another reader whose reading of Shakespeare 'washes over' and enriches their own. If, as Lamarque and Olsen suggest, 'the twin perspectives of imaginative involvement and awareness of artifice are both indispensable in an appropriate response to works of fiction,' it would seem that these students are indeed 'attend[ing] twice at once' on both a personal and critical level (Andrews 2001: 89). Andrews goes on to draw attention to Hawkins' belief that 'identity for readers of all ages is partly affected by the books they encounter, and that the books themselves are part of conversations that have been influenced by existing literature and cultural histories. Works that interleave, as it were, echoes of other works and (by implication) other cultures, other voices – these represent the hybrid nature of contemporary identities' (Andrews 2001: 91).

Assessing the students' performance: Stage 2: formative assessment and differentiation in practice

Reflection Activity 5.3

Based on the second transcript cited earlier, consider how you might use this assessment data to plan for the future learning of one or more of the four students. In terms of individual personalized learning, consider differentiating by task, menu, pace, resource or interest. You may wish to refer back to Chapter 1 here.

Orla

It is noticeable how Orla begins to broaden her outlook and extend her thinking as the discussion develops. In Vygotskian terms, it is clear that the assessment process itself (i.e. the class discussion) has enormously extended Orla's ability to work with the text; referring again to Anderson and Krathwohl's taxonomy, she is now *classifying, summarizing, inferring, comparing, analysing, evaluating, differentiating* and *critiquing*; speaking of Shakespeare's move away from 'taut plots' in his late plays, Orla connects this with not only the 1940s date of MacNeice's poem but also aspects of the dramatic form; 'Sort of like in the future, isn't it? Not like all those period dramas.' It would be useful to use her apparent interest here to suggest some wider critical reading around the dramatic genre; moreover, her positive response to this shared learning activity suggest Orla could develop her knowledge and skills further by participating in an extended group research project leading to the *creating* of a presentation. In Orla's case, independent learning need not mean individual learning, as the process of the task may well be as important as the content.

Rachel

The later stages of the group discussion provide further evidence of Rachel's capacity to work with texts in sophisticated, perceptive and creative ways. Like Orla, she quotes from MacNeice's *Autolycus* – a text she has never seen before – to illustrate her points, but she goes beyond this to use the poem to enrich her understanding of the complex nature of the romance genre of *The Winter's Tale*. Rachel suggests that MacNeice is 'talking about Shakespeare predominantly in the poem and he also takes a step back and looks at the play as, well, it's this kind of jumble of 'tapestried romance' – and using 'tapestried' makes it sound rich and varied and quite – of Shakespeare's age. "Classical bric-a-brac" . . . "grottos" – he says this is something Shakespeare put together like a hotchpotch.' Using Anderson and Krathwohl's taxonomy, Rachel's realignment of elements of her existing knowledge is evidence of her ability to *attribute* and *critique* autonomously to *create* a new pattern of ideas.

In order to consolidate her *creating,* the most challenging mental function in the revised taxonomy of learning, an appropriate task for Rachel might require her to explore her awareness of genre, context and the intricacies of language through a piece of transformative writing. Such a task, which unifies creative and critical textual approaches, could help Rachel to first consolidate her higher-order thinking skills as she first *evaluates* and *critiques* the decisions writers face when producing texts before intervening in the text itself. Working with her primary source text, *The Winter's Tale,* or indeed MacNeice's *Autolycus* – already a 'transformed' version of the original in a sense – Rachel can *generate, plan* and *produce* a new scene, speech or stanza, retell part of the story from an alternative viewpoint or change the genre; in order to do so, she must read and re-read her source texts both actively and imaginatively. This type of task encourages students to produce an original written response which remains rooted convincingly within their source text, a hands-on approach, which complements more formal academic approaches to the study of English literature and invites the student writer to ask, as Chris Thurgar-Dawson does, 'how has my own rewriting of the text enabled me to see the decisions that the original writer took?' He argues that in higher education 'your answers to this question complete the learning cycle and will demonstrate how far you have come as a "writing reader"' (2008: 25). Transformative writing is now a required coursework element of the revised UK A-level English Literature specifications introduced in 2009 which encompasses the government's new emphasis on 'creativity'; it allows students to explore alternative ways of responding to literary texts and practise a range of close and wide reading skills. Rachel will have to know how her chosen source text works before trying to re-create aspects of it, so from a practical standpoint her learning journey will involve a sequence of challenging creative decisions as she reshapes characters, events and ideas from the source material to show her knowledge of literary genre, narrative structure and setting (Onyett 2008: 13).

Heather

Like Rachel, Heather can also reorganize elements of her knowledge; we see her *differentiating* and *critiquing* when she discovers a new way of thinking about *The Winter's Tale* by connecting it with her pre-existing knowledge of *Romeo and Juliet*, a text she had studied more than two years earlier. Juliet, she argues, is 'playing out a story that's been written for her' whereas Perdita is 'driving her own story'. Heather then further refines her ideas, achieving a high level of technical and critical awareness as she begins to consider 'the difference between feminist views of them'. In terms of planning for Heather's individual learning needs, this information suggests that we might differentiate for her in terms of interest and text by getting her to *critique* a challenging secondary text such as Lisa Jardine's 1983 study *Still Harping on Daughters: Women and Drama in the Age of Shakespeare*. This should help Heather to extend the range of ideas with which to grapple as she continues to *create* independent textual readings of her own.

Lucy

In assessing Lucy's learning needs, we might start with the significant fact that her first – rather tentative – statement is not really picked up by the other students when she wonders whether MacNeice was addressing Autolycus in the final stanza; 'I thought he was.' When Orla argues against her interpretation, she backs down straight away: 'Oh yes.' If Lucy were to assess her own progress at this point, it seems likely she would see herself as less competent than her peers – which, given her initial reluctance to participate, is probably a belief she brought with her to the lesson. However, the teacher intervenes to draw Lucy into the centre of the shared talk space and place her on equal terms with the other students by logging one of Lucy's points and waiting for a relevant moment to reintroduce it: 'I want to go back to what you said, Lucy.'

This purposeful invitation to speak models for the rest of the group the need to value her contributions.

Managing classroom talk in this way allows the teacher to assess Lucy's understanding and encourage her to take more responsibility for her own learning. The open question, 'What do you think he means there, Lucy?,' is enough to ensure all four students begin to see her as a potentially successful learner. Lucy's peers learn that working with ideas collaboratively can lead to a wide-ranging shared corpus of knowledge; as both Heather and Orla respond to Lucy's ideas and in so doing extend their own, we see clear evidence of literature being made available to a community of learners learning from each other.

It is always worth thinking about which students we choose to answer our questions and indeed why we are asking them in the first place. Do we ask those who catch our eye, because they are constantly within our sightlines when the classroom seating plan leaves other students to all intents and purposes invisible to us? Or do we choose the most able in order to elicit a reliably high-quality response which will model good work to the others, or the most troublesome, because it is a way of calling them to account for going off-task? If so, we need to move the students, move the chairs or move ourselves and think of a way of targeting questions more successfully, whether it be throwing a ball, passing a conch or pulling names out of a hat. As may be seen from the group work which underpins this chapter, our questioning technique needs careful structuring and ongoing self-evaluation; on several occasions the teacher stops to reframe statements as questions: 'the implication is . . . well, how does that link in with the rest of the play, do you think?' Using open or Socratic questions to structure classroom talk is undoubtedly hard to manage; it may be something of a cliché to say that the best question a teacher can ask is the one to which he or she does not already know the answer, but there are a wide range of factors to be considered before that stage is reached.

The powerful learning environment created in this classroom context shows the value of appropriately scaffolding the student's response. After initially seeming reluctant to contribute, Lucy begins to experiment with new ideas and methods, *comparing* Autolycus with other outcasts from mainstream Elizabethan society, 'Thieves, prostitutes'. When the teacher adds 'vagabonds' to her list, Lucy trumps this with 'ruined maids'. This contribution is evidence of an ability to *exemplify, summarize, infer* and even *differentiate* it would have been hard to predict earlier, given Lucy's shaky start; she has, in fact, *generated* an independent, creative and imaginative link with a poem she had read several months earlier, Thomas Hardy's *The Ruined Maid*. When she reminds

Orla of previous challenges the group had faced together and overcome, 'It's hard at first isn't it, working it out – like the Brontë poems,' we have very clear evidence of metacognition; in *checking* and *critiquing* their previous learning, Lucy is learning about learning. By the end of the classroom discussion, Lucy has a very different view of her own potential. Though initially reluctant and insecure, she makes confident contributions which develop points raised by others and engages with two complex and challenging literary texts with insight and pleasure.

In order to plan for Lucy's future learning, it is useful to note the confident way in which she comes to *summarize* different phases and aspects of her learning by *organizing* her pre-existing intertextual and historical knowledge. Given how well she handled MacNeice's reworking of Shakespeare, if we were to differentiate by text or interest for Lucy, setting her to reverse the process and look at how (and why) Shakespeare reworked *his* source text, Robert Greene's *Pandosto*, or *The Triumph of Time*, would seem an appropriate task; so, too, would investigating the famous historical and contextual oddities and anomalies of *The Winter's Tale*.

Formative assessment of the type modelled here can provide information about students which cannot be gained by marking individual written tasks. The students might have been given MacNeice's poem to write about silently and alone, but even had they been asked the relatively 'open' questions they worked with orally in class, no written question could have tapped into those hidden reservoirs of knowledge about the Elizabethan Poor Law, feminist criticism or Adolf Hitler, or encouraged them to make intertextual connections to other texts they had previously studied, from *Romeo and Juliet* to Victorian poetry. Moreover, as noted in Chapter 1, the differentiated learning pathways which have been suggested for each student on the basis of the assessment activity all lead back to the text itself and we would expect the subsequent knowledge gained by them all to be pooled and shared with the rest of the class.

Thus, the core assessment activity here – using MacNeice's poem as a way into a consideration of his role and function in *The Winter's Tale* – may be used by the teacher to direct individual students towards appropriately differentiated tasks selected from a rich menu of follow-up activities. Arguably more important than what the teacher learns from any such activity, however, is whether or not it offers the students themselves the chance to participate in an ongoing process of peer and self-assessment, judging and evaluating their own learning and that of their colleagues. One of the benefits of this kind of oral assessment task is that because it makes students take more responsibility for their own learning the teacher can draw back from the discussion at times in order to observe what learning is taking place and think about how, when (and if) to intervene. It is often hard to establish the relative contributions of the members of a group, particularly if only the product or outcome of the work is assessed; therefore, observing (and occasionally recording) students speaking and listening must be handled carefully to ensure it fulfils our assessment brief and really does tell us things which can't be measured by written tests. Nevertheless, working with Rachel, Orla, Heather and Lucy in this way has provided information about their individual strategies for attacking previously unseen literary texts, how they see themselves as learners, how they work in teams and the extent to which they can build on the ideas of others. Using this knowledge it is now possible to provide high-quality differentiated feedback and plan appropriately differentiated follow up activities.

Never the twain? Bridging the gap between formative and summative assessment

The famous 1944 Education Act legislated for one of the most hard-edged forms of summative assessment ever seen in the United Kingdom in the form of the so-called 'scholarship' or '11-plus', a socially and culturally divisive process the comic satirist John O'Farrell lampoons as 'a bit like the sorting hat in Harry Potter: if you looked better in a cloth cap, you were designated working class and sent off to learn about metalwork and burglary. And if the bowler hat was a better fit, then you were clearly middle class and were destined to study English, Maths and fiddling your tax expenses' (O'Farrell 2009: 59). In her mordantly witty autobiography *Bad Blood* (2000) the feminist literary critic Lorna Sage recalls her primary education at Hanmer village school on the Welsh–English border in the early 1950s and in particular the eccentric approach to assessment of the head teacher, Mr Palmer. As Sage remarks laconically, on the day of the 11-plus examination his methods were, as usual, notably unorthodox:

> When my time came, Mr Palmer graciously cheated me through. Strolling past my desk on his invigilation rounds, he trailed a plump finger down my page of sums, pointed significantly at several, then crossed two fingers behind his back as he walked away. So I did those again.
>
> Perhaps the record of failure was starting to look fishy. The world was changing, education was changing, and the notion that school should reflect your ready-made place in the world was going out of fashion even in Hanmer. It was against the grain to acknowledge this, though. The cause of hierarchy and

immobility was served by singling out the few children whose families didn't fit and setting them homework. Mr Palmer drew the line at marking it, however. The three of us were given sums to do, then told to compare the results in a corner next morning. If all three, or two of us, arrived at the same answer then that was the correct one. If – as often happened – all three of us produced different answers then that particular long division or fraction retreated into the realms of undecidability . . . it was never part of Mr Palmer's plan (the school's plan) to reveal that the necessary skills were *learnable*. If you passed the scholarship, that was because you were somebody who should never have been at Hanmer school in the first place, was his theory. (Sage 2000: 20–1)

Thus Mr Palmer differentiates by task, while Lorna and her two friends participate in a primitive and blackly comic form of peer assessment. As defined by Topping, peer assessment is 'an arrangement in which individuals consider the amount, level, value, worth, quality, or successfulness of the products or outcomes of learning of others of similar status' (Topping 1998: 249). Unfortunately, because it was not 'part of Mr Palmer's plan (the school's plan) to reveal that the necessary skills were *learnable*', the trio were being tested on skills they had yet to master (and in Lorna's case never would) and had no idea how to evaluate their work in any case.

Today, as we have seen earlier in this chapter, teachers can plan peer assessment activities which enable groups to share the workload fairly, take individual and collective responsibility for their work and evaluate the contributions of all members; while the phrase 'put your pens down' may be most closely associated with an instruction to candidates at the end of a written examination, it might be better directed at teachers who still persist with a red-ink approach to marking. Although feedback will always be oral and comment-based in the context of the type of classroom assessment activity we have seen in this chapter, as Butler and others have shown, marks and grades tend to override even detailed and helpful comments for students; therefore, it is usually best to avoid summative assessment when the primary goal is to redefine specific learning targets (Black 2004: 5). Extensive research has shown the negative impact of summative assessment on student motivation. Some of the most powerful points to emerge include lowered self-esteem among pupils who have performed badly in a test, despite no previous correlation between self-esteem and achievement, the emergence of an assessment culture which promotes 'extrinsic' motivation in terms of rewards such as merits or certificates rather than the 'intrinsic' motivation of enjoying learning and an increased level of anxiety among students and teachers. Yet summative assessment is a fact of life, and we must acknowledge the impact upon teaching and learning of the kind of high-stakes culture of assessment in which league tables, value-added results and contextual data are part of the discourse among parents in the playground as well as teachers in the staffroom in ways which would have been unimaginable even 20 years ago. 'You go to a parents' evening,' noted one English teacher in 2005. 'I will tell them what level [their child] is working at and they ask, "but what will they get in the test?" As if somehow this was far more reliable than my teacher assessment' (Black et al. 2007: 5). Undoubtedly Rachel, Orla, Heather and Lucy – and their parents – will want to know what grades they are expected to get when they complete their literary studies, and this information is vital when applying to UK higher education institutions which base their offers on the grades predicted by applicants' teachers months in advance of the official publication of their examination results. Nevertheless, while scattergun decontextualized tests do little to indicate what students really know, the kind of ongoing formative assessment modelled in this chapter can, over time, enable us to evaluate their progress sensitively and accurately. Moreover, Daw's study of schools achieving high examination results in Suffolk, England, noted (among other factors) a commitment to 'balanced teaching approaches which enable exposition, exegesis and exploration to take place' and the provision of 'models of high-quality critical discussion' such as that we saw earlier in this chapter (Andrews 2001: 97).

Any external testing regime has to both enforce and support the parameters of the subject under scrutiny, but within the classroom context we need to think about what any assessment system we use is actually measuring – the amount of learning which has already happened or the amount of learning which is still to be done. As Paul Black points out, in the United Kingdom, ever since the inception of the National Curriculum in the late 1980s, although the involvement of teachers in the assessment process originally indicated that teacher assessment 'could serve both formative and summative functions', in practice this has not happened. Some teachers still equate assessment with assigning marks, levels and grades aimed at satisfying the demands of the government, senior management, parents and employers rather than reframing it as a tool which can help us find out what students know or still need to know. Moreover, even though some teachers have managed to square the assessment circle and 'integrate both formative and summative functions effectively . . . the emphasis has been on maximizing test scores rather than meeting students' learning needs'; Black notes that the government's 'trust in formal tests as an engine of change has led to pupils in England stealing from the United States the dubious distinction of being the most frequently tested in the world' (Black 2005: 252, 259). Even though there has been an increased emphasis in UK schools and colleges in the past decade on the kinds of formative assessment which take place in the classroom, there undoubtedly remains an often uneasy mutual relationship between this and the summative assessment associated with public examinations which leads Black to wonder whether we, as classroom practitioners, can ever really bridge the gap between assessment *for* learning and the assessment *of* learning; whether, indeed, 'their mutual contradictions and inconsistencies simply make more clear to us that there are, and always will be, hard choices with far less room for manoeuvre than we imagine' (Black 2001: 66). Squaring this circle as far as we can is perhaps the major challenge we face on behalf of our students.

Discourse and practice: models of assessment and 'assessment awareness'

Acquiring an assured working knowledge of assessment discourses and practices is a challenging ongoing process for teachers. Harlen et al. (2004) have found evidence of bias in teacher assessments such as well-behaved girls getting higher grades than do badly behaved boys for the same quality of work, or students with special needs being marked inaccurately due to low expectations or even a misplaced sense of kindness (Harlen et al. 2004 in Gardner 2007: 19). Yet as Gardner notes, it seems 'bias and error may be significantly reduced or even corrected by a combination of training and moderation. There is also evidence that involving teachers in developing and setting criteria can considerably reduce bias and error.' He goes on to quantify the necessary assessment expertise teachers need in terms of three complementary elements: assessment literacy, skills and values (Gardner 2007: 19). According to Gardner, assessment literacy would include knowledge of the types, methods and purposes of assessment, and an understanding of the reliability and validity of assessment results, the interpretation of responses, scores and grades, and so on, and their implications for learners. Assessment skills would in turn include competence in different assessment methods, question design, item writing, feedback, moderation, facilitation of self and peer assessment and so on. Assessment values would include an endorsement of the importance of consistency, impartiality and transparency in assessment practice. (2007: 19)

It is now nearly 20 years since the abolition of the popular 100% coursework option for the UK's General Certificate of Secondary Education (GCSE) examination taken by most pupils in their final year of compulsory schooling. Given current levels of concern about plagiarism and the extent to which some parents may be 'helping' their children with assignments out of school, it seems very unlikely that this 'pure' strain of active teacher assessment will ever be revived in the United Kingdom; indeed from 2010, coursework tasks will be replaced by controlled tests administered wholly within class time. Nevertheless, there is still extensive support available to help classroom practitioners extend their professional assessment expertise in the form of the standardization materials and support meetings provided by the examination boards, with best practice disseminated via a chained sequence of internal and external moderation processes. The usual procedure is for teachers to mark their own students' work and then check their application of the relevant criteria has been consistent and appropriate by comparing it with that of their colleagues within school. Samples are then moderated externally by trained experts (often also practising teachers themselves) to verify the application of the nationally agreed standard. Arguably even more valuable is the parallel system of area consensus moderation organized by the AQA (Assessment and Qualifications Alliance) which validates the assessment practices of a consortium of local schools and colleges who collectively review each other's work. This process not only confirms the final marks awarded to individual students in terms of the external awarding process but also allows other classroom practitioners to review the professional judgment of the original teacher-assessor. By observing how other subject specialists have taught and assessed *their* students, this process can often consolidate a positive and confident sense of assessment ownership.

In 2009 the centre-right think-tank Reform reviewed the cherished talisman of the UK's summative assessment system, arguing that since the replacement in 2000 of the traditional linear terminal examination with a pattern of modular units, the GCE A-level had been 'dumbed down'. The modular system is characterized as rewarding pupils who have been drilled to jump through a narrowly prescriptive sequence of 'assessment objectives') which do not really show what it means to be good at the subject and have helped to produce an undergraduate cohort often incapable of independent thought. Reform also criticizes those teachers who spoon-feed students in order to ensure they achieve the limited and restrictive targets imposed by the assessment objectives. The Reform critique may be overstated, but it provides a useful context in which to consider some profound implications for both the external system of summative assessment and also the types of formative assessment we work with in the classroom.

Looking back a quarter of a century or more, 'doing English' often meant working with canonical texts at the heart of which were apparently buried priceless nuggets of meaning; many teachers explained the significance of texts to their students rather than helping them make meanings of their own. Asked what they had learned during the two years of advanced-level study which preceded university, they might well have listed the classic canonical texts they had 'done' without questioning why some writers were 'major' and others were 'modern' or why so few texts were written by women or anyone whose first language was not English. They probably wouldn't have asked why all examinations took the same format – 3-hour closed-book papers – and were often unable to independently interrogate their texts because they lacked any critical framework with which to do so. Lacan, Foucault, Kristeva and Barthes might have been deconstructing the very notion of the text for 15 years or more in France, but many students (and probably many long-serving teachers) had never heard of any of them.

In the twenty-first century, a top-down transmission approach is no longer workable in terms of teaching, learning or assessment. Modern literature courses place much less emphasis upon gaining an encyclopaedic knowledge of a small number of set texts than on acquiring a range of close and wider reading practices and ways of thinking which will equip students for future study and provide valuable transferable skills. Fortunately, too, most teachers now feel at ease with a constructivist approach to teaching and learning in which students are active agents in the learning process rather than passive recipients, and as Black et al. note, this means that the 'learning environment has to be "engineered" to involve pupils more actively in the tasks. The emphasis has to be on the pupils doing the thinking and making that thinking public' (Black et al. 2004: 10). The teacher's role is to ensure that each student understands the nature of the learning taking place in the classroom and can work with others to make progress, no longer 'presenter of content' but 'leader of an exploration and development of ideas in which all [students are] involved' (Black et al. 2004: 10). Once more the relevance of David Kolb's belief in the need for a variety of flexible teacher 'roles' is underlined. Moreover, even when there is core curriculum content to be presented to our students, it is, after all, as easy to publish a PowerPoint presentation on the school intranet or VLE after the lesson which allows them to read, edit and recreate their own versions as it is to leave them passive receivers of our boundless wisdom.

That this kind of active partnership approach to teaching, learning and assessment is both more productive and more enjoyable is self-evident, yet teachers and students must still collaborate in an assessment process in which the eventual outcome still includes at least one substantial externally assessed examination. Yet even here one may see some potentially good news; the new UK A-level specifications from 2010 were developed according to government guidelines designed to encourage independent research, open-ended questions and more detailed responses. In this context, preparing students for external examinations via a 'death by essay plan' system cannot be pedagogically sound if it not only disadvantages those who do not benefit from such didactic strategies but also leaves many students underprepared for the challenges of further or higher education. The four key assessment objectives common to all current UK A-level English Literature courses explicitly state that students will be expected to:

- articulate creative, informed and relevant responses to literary texts, using appropriate terminology and concepts, and coherent, accurate written expression
- demonstrate detailed critical in analysing the ways in which form, structure and language shape meanings in literary texts
- explore connections and comparisons between different literary texts, informed by interpretations of other readers
- demonstrate understanding of the significance and influence of the contexts in which literary texts are written and received.

Yet alongside ensuring that students master this set of core skills, teachers need to engineer a flexible and exploratory learning environment which prepares young learners not only for terminal examinations, where outcomes are finite, inevitable and measurable, but also for the wider world of work, where outcomes are often much less clear-cut. In this context it is interesting to note that while there has been a marked widening of the range of assessment methods used in UK higher education institutions over the past few years which is expanding exponentially in response to the demands of a larger and more diverse body of students at tertiary level, there has been relatively little change in the format of public examinations. Contrary to Reform's suggestion, the UK's shift towards modularization from the traditional linear system has more to do with the timing of summative assessment than its essential characteristics.

Examination success has always depended upon not only the extent to which students have mastered the course content but also how adept they are in producing a highly specific type of written response with a complex set of internal discourse structures and conventions (otherwise known as the traditional literary-critical essay) under stressful sudden-death conditions. Classroom-based assessment for learning activities, on the other hand, help us work out what and how students learn and plan our teaching accordingly. If we visualize an assessment cline or continuum, we need to acknowledge that its summative end is beyond our control – even if, like Gardner, we might be tempted to ask why, if teachers are trusted to teach, we need 'externally administered tests to assess the results of their teaching? Surely assessment is just as much a part of teaching as it is of learning. Do we bat an eyelid at college or university teachers judging the performance of their own students?' (Gardner 2007: 18). There is much anecdotal evidence to suggest students emerging from the United Kingdom's relentless assessment regime are now looking closely at the assessment methods to which they will be subject when selecting their higher education courses, so perhaps we should look to the learners rather than the teachers when evaluating current assessment discourses and practices. The United Kingdom's National Union of Students' *Principles of Effective Assessment* (2009) states that effective assessment:

- should be for learning, not simply of learning
- should be reliable, valid, fair and consistent
- should consist of effective and constructive feedback
- should be innovative and have the capacity to inspire and motivate
- should measure understanding and application, rather than technique and memory
- should be conducted throughout the course, rather than being positioned as a final event
- should develop key skills such as peer and reflective assessment
- should be central; to staff development and teaching strategies, and frequently reviewed
- should be of a manageable amount for both tutors and students
- should encourage dialogue between students and their tutors and students and their peers. (Attwood 2009: 34)

In practice, while universities have more freedom than schools to set up their own internal assessment methodologies and many undergraduates submit a project or dissertation in lieu of a terminal examination, exam papers can be much easier to mark than, say, wikis, blogs, oral presentations or group work, as well as being open to external verification or challenge. Dai Hounsell argues that terminal examinations are a throwback to a pre-computer age, requiring students to demonstrate writing skills largely irrelevant to a world in which we work on PCs which allow us to draft, proofread and edit over a substantial length of time. Written exams can show how well students can marshal a logical argument or balance a debate, but this may tell more about how effectively they have mastered the specifics of formal examination discourse than about the extent of their subject knowledge. Moreover, Hounsell argues, since most students are not going into jobs where this kind of writing will ever be needed, this system of assessment may no longer be practical, functional or constructive (Attwood 2009: 36).

Teaching, learning and assessment: towards an integrated approach

The assessment decisions teachers make both collectively and individually within their own classrooms are crucial. It is necessary to draw upon a portfolio of assessment tasks and approaches which are formative in nature while simultaneously familiarizing students with the demands of the system of external summative assessment, since their exam results will permanently define a key aspect of their educational achievement for parents, higher education institutions and employers. The assessment principles we adopt model for our students powerful and pervasive attitudes to learning, and thus should be valid and reliable in reflecting accurately and fairly the content and delivery of a particular scheme of work.

When learning goals rather than test scores are prioritized, a wide repertoire of knowledge and skills might be incorporated within a summative assessment activity, whether the aim is to gauge students' progress with regard to a week's work, a semester's or a year's. Peer and self-assessment may be included in summative reports or records, and students' learning can be measured across a range of in-class activities rather than by a sudden-death written examination. Assessing the work of each student in a large class every lesson is clearly impossible, but if we did attempt it – by constantly setting and marking short pieces of written work, for example – we would often measure the teaching which has taken place rather than the learning.

On the other hand, from a purely logistical point of view, written tests and examinations are in many ways easier to manage than the type of formative oral assessment which has been modelled in this chapter. To assess the learning needs of a whole class in this way would encompass a number of lessons and/or tutorials and careful notes would have to be kept on individual rates and levels of progress. To establish such a model of regular, differentiated, ongoing formative assessment is undeniably challenging, but if it is possible, to quote Jonothan Neelands once again, 'with this group . . . in this space . . . in the time I have available', then it will be more productive, more personalized and more reliable than random 'hit-and-run' paper tests (1984: 9). Moreover external summative assessment can lead to a pressure-cooker culture which encourages students to ask not, as the Victorian poet and critic Matthew Arnold did, 'What does this mean to me?' but instead 'How do I get the best grade?' Before long, a classroom culture of potentially productive peer assessment may be reduced to students finding out what others got for an assignment and obsessively gauging this arbitrary standard against their own performance. The kind of classroom talk which has been the focus of this chapter, however, while undoubtedly demanding to organize, manage and capture, does offer both teachers and – crucially – students, a powerful way of assessing for learning which is designed into our schemes of work rather than bolted on at the end.

Since our aim is to promote productive links between formative and summative assessment by encouraging students to become confident assessors of their own work and that of others, we do well to bear in mind that when feedback is summative (grade- or mark-based) rather than formative (comment-based), weaker students can develop what Carol Dweck has termed 'learned helplessness', that is, a self-perceived inability to overcome failure (1986: 1040). When the classroom assessment culture prioritizes competitive testing over collaborative learning, there is often a negative impact on students' motivation and self-esteem which in turn adversely affects their capacity to acquire new skills. Over time a de-skilling effect can emerge which impacts particularly harshly on weaker students who tend to ascribe their 'failure' to a lack of ability, over which they have little or no control, rather than a lack of effort, which they can put right. Thus, the learning goals we set for our pupils can influence not only how they see themselves as learners but also how effectively they learn (Dweck 1986: 1040). We might think Lucy, whom we met earlier in this chapter, was in danger of this when she responded to the unthreatening open question, 'What do you think, Lucy?', with a panicked, 'Oh no. I actually don't know! Can you come back to me in five minutes?' However, because the assessment context here was collaborative and comment-based, as opposed to competitive and grade-based, a full-blown attack of 'learned helplessness' was avoided.

Sooner rather than later, however, Lucy has to learn about the specific format and demands of her final examinations. Since repeated timed tests are largely ineffective in terms of developing higher-order thinking skills, we must facilitate more creative and autonomous approaches to exam preparation; one practical activity is to explore examination assessment criteria, question papers and mark schemes with students so they can use these materials as templates to create their own versions. Then again, if students complete self-evaluation sheets and submit them together with pieces of work to be marked, feedback can be tailored to specific requests for help or perceived areas of concern and differentiated follow-up activities set. While no one (least of all our students) will thank us for adopting a pedagogical approach which leaves them unprepared for their final examinations, there is substantial evidence to show that an impoverished diet of teaching to the test is counterproductive. Thus, our assessment discourses and practices need to be linked to the attitudes, concepts and skills we wish students to acquire and the ways in which their success (or lack thereof) will be externally measured; aligning our classroom practice with the demands of the terminal examinations allows students to become assessment-literate, planning their own learning based on a clear understanding of how the system works.

At present, given our relative powerlessness with regard to the modes and methods of summative assessment, innovation in classroom practice must stem from our use of formative assessment techniques. Rachel, Orla, Heather and Lucy must be able to compare and contrast a wide range of texts, and to do so they need to investigate and assimilate a vast amount of material and prioritize their workload effectively. In order to make autonomous textual meanings while considering alternative points of view they must be open-minded and flexible, weighing up and evaluating opposing arguments and thinking on their feet. To explore contexts of both production and reception and reflect on the ways in which texts contain encoded cultural ideas and values they need to be able to spot hidden and multiple meanings. All this suggests that if students are to be judged on how they think as well as on what they know, a top-down transmissive approach to teaching, learning and assessment will be stiflingly obstructive. We need to reframe assessment as an integral part of the learning cycle as opposed to a sword of Damocles waiting to fall upon our students at the end of their learning journey.

References

Abbs, P. (1982) *English Within the Arts: A Radical Alternative for English and the Arts in the Curriculum.* London, Sydney, Auckland, Toronto: Hodder and Stoughton.

Aciman, A. and Rensin, E. (2009) *Twitterature.* London: Penguin.

Alexander, R. (2005) 'Culture, dialogue and learning: notes on an emerging pedagogy.' *Education, Culture and Cognition: intervening for growth.* International Association for Cognitive Education and Psychology (IACEP) 10th International Conference, University of Durham, UK, 10–14 July.

Almond, D. (1998) *Skellig.* London: Hodder Children's Books.

Anderson, L. W. (Ed.), Krathwohl, D. R. (Ed.), Airasian, P.W., Cruikshank, K. A., Mayer, R. E., Pintrich, P. R., Raths, J., & Wittrock, M. C. (2001). *A taxonomy for learning, teaching, and assessing: A revision of Bloom's Taxonomy of Educational Objectives.* New York: Longman.

Andrews, R. (2001) *Teaching and Learning English: A Guide to Recent Research and its Applications.* London and New York: Continuum.

Arnold, M. (1975) 'General Report for the Year 1880', in M. Mathieson, *The Preachers of Culture,* London: George Allen and Unwin.

Arnold, R. (1991) *Writing Development.* Milton Keynes: Open University Press.

Asher, S. and Williams, G. (1987) *Children's Social Development: Information for Parents and Teachers.* Urbana and Champaign: University of Illinois Press.

Attwood, R (2009) 'Well, What Do You Know?' *Times Higher Educational Supplement,* 29 January, http://www.timeshighereducation.co.uk/story.asp?storyCode=405152&sectioncode=26 (accessed 29/06/09).

Barker, R. G. (1968) *Ecological psychology: concepts and methods for studying the environment of human behavior.* Stanford, CA: Stanford University Press.

Barker, R. G. (1980) 'This week's citation classic'. *Citation Classics,* 26, 30 June http://www.garfield. library.upenn.edu/classics1980/A1980JW15800001.pdf (accessed 23/01/10).

Barthes, R. (1977) *Image Music Text.* London: Fontana.

Bassett, D., Cawston, T., Thraves, L. and Truss, E. (2009) 'A New Level', http://www.reform.co.uk/ Research/ResearchArticles/tabid/82/smid/378/ArticleID/772/reftab/56/t/A%20new%20level/ Default.aspx (accessed 29/06/09).

Beadle, P. (2006a) 'Mixed Abilities', *The Guardian,* 17 January.

Beadle, P. (2006b) 'Personalised Learning? I'd rather be a 60s throwback', *The Guardian,* 21 February.

Berne, E. (1964) *Games People Play: The Basic Handbook of Transactional Analysis.* New York: Ballantine Books.

Bernstein B. (1996) *Pedagogy, symbolic control and identity.* London: Taylor & Francis.

Black, P. (2001) 'Dreams, Strategies and Systems: portraits of assessment past, present and future', *Assessment in Education* 8, 1, 65–85.

Black, P. and Wiliam, D. (2005) 'Lessons from around the world: how policies, politics and cultures constrain and afford assessment practices', *Curriculum Journal,* 16, 2, 249–261.

Black, P., Harrison, C., Hodgen. J, Marshall, B. and Serret, N. (2007) 'Riding the Interface: an exploration of the issues that beset teachers as they strive for assessment systems', http://www.kcl.ac.uk/content/1/c6/01/54/36/Ridingtheinterface.pdf (accessed 15/12/09).

Bloom, B. S., Engelhart, M. D., Furst, E. J., Hill, W. H., and Krathwohl, D. R. (1956) *Taxonomy of educational objectives: The classification of educational goals. Handbook 1: Cognitive domain.* New York: David McKay.

Bowers, C. A. (1977) 'Emergent ideological characteristics of educational policy', *Teachers College Record,* 79, 1, 33–54.

Bronfenbrenner, U. (1979) *The Ecology of Human Development: Experiments by Nature or Design.* Cambridge MA: Harvard University Press.

Brown, A. L. and Ferrara, R. A. (1985) 'Diagnosing zones of proximal development', in J. Wertsch (Ed.) *Culture, Communication, and Cognition: Vygotskian Perspectives.* New York: Cambridge University Press.

Bruner, J. (1986) *Actual Minds, Possible Worlds,* Cambridge MA and London England: Harvard University Press.

Bruner, J. (1996) *The Culture of Education.* Cambridge, MA: Harvard University Press.

Bullough, R. V. and Goldstein, S. L. (1984) 'Technical curriculum form and American elementary-school art education', *Journal of Curriculum Studies,* 16, 2, 143–154.

Canfield, J. V. and Donnell, F. H. (eds) (1964) *Readings in the Theory of Knowledge.* New York: Appleton-Century-Crofts.

Carleheden, M. (2006) 'Towards democratic foundations: a Habermasian perspective on the politics of education'. *Journal of Curriculum Studies,* 3, 5, 521–543.

Coffield, F. J. Moseley, D. V. Hall, E. and Ecclestone, K. (2004a) *Should we be using learning styles? What research has to say to practice.* London: Learning and Skills Research Centre / University of Newcastle upon Tyne.

Coffield, F. J. Moseley, D. V. Hall, E. and Ecclestone, K. (2004b) *Learning styles and pedagogy in post-16 learning: a systematic and critical review.* London: Learning and Skills Research Centre / University of Newcastle upon Tyne.

Corcoran, N. (2009) 'Heaney and Yeats', in B. O'Donoghue (Ed.) *Seamus Heaney.* Cambridge: University Press.

Cox, B. (1991) *Cox on Cox: An English Curriculum for the 1990s.* London: Hodder & Stoughton.

DCSF (2008) *Autumn Performance Report 2008: Progress against Public Service Agreements.* Runcorn: Public Communications Unit.

DCSF (2009) *The National Strategies Secondary English subject leader development materials – Autumn 2009.* London: HMSO.

DCSF (2010) *Thinking Skills in Primary Classrooms* http://www.standards.dfes.gov.uk/thinkingskills/ (accessed 30/01/10).

De Bono, E. (2000) *Six Thinking Hats.* London: Penguin.

De Corte, E., Verschaffel, L. Entwistle, N. and van Merriënboer, J. (2003) (eds) *Powerful Learning Environments: Unravelling Basic Components and Dimensions.* Oxford: Elsevier Science.

Dewey, J. (1910) *How We Think.* Lexington, MA: D.C. Heath.

Dixon, J. (1967) *Growth Through English.* Oxford: Oxford University Press.

Dweck, C. (1986) 'Motivational processes affecting learning', *American Psychologist*, 41, 10, 1040–1048.

Everest, C. (2003) 'Differentiation is just another pressure meted out by managers', *The Guardian,* 18 February.

Ewert, G. D. (1991) 'Habermas and Education: A Comprehensive Overview of the Influence of Habermas in Educational Literature'. *Review of Educational Research,* 61, 3, 345–378.

Eysenck, H. (2000). *Intelligence: A New Look*. Transaction Publishers.

Fish, S. (1980) *Is There a Text in This Class? The Authority of Interpretive Communities.* Cambridge, MA: Harvard University Press.

Fisher, R. (2000) *Teaching Thinking: Philosophical Enquiry in the Classroom*. London: Continuum.

Gardner, J. (2007) "Is teaching a 'partial' profession?", *Make the Grade*, Summer 2007, CIEA, http://www.ciea.org.uk/upload/PDFs/summer_2007/debate.pdf (accessed 29/06/09).

Gibson, J. J. (1977) 'The Theory of Affordances', in R. Shaw and J. Bransford, (eds) *Perceiving, Acting, and Knowing*. Hillsdale, NJ: Erlbaum.

Goleman, D. (1996) *Emotional Intelligence: Why It Can Matter More Than IQ*. London: Bloomsbury.

Goodwyn, A. (1992) 'English Teachers and the Cox Models', *English in Education*, 28, 3, 4–10.

Graves, D. (1983) *Writing: Teachers and Children at Work*. Portsmouth, New Hampshire: Heinemann Educational Books.

Griffith, P. (1987) *Literary Theory and English Teaching*. Milton Keynes: Open University Press.

Guilford, J. P. (1967) *The nature of human intelligence*. New York: McGraw-Hill.

Habermas, J. (1996) *Between Facts and Norms: Contributions to a Discourse Theory of Law and Democracy,* trans. W. Rehg. Cambridge: Polity Press.

Hardman, F. (2001) 'What Do We Mean by Secondary English Teaching?', in J. Williamson, M. Fleming, F. Hardman and D. Stevens, *Meeting the Standards in Secondary English: A Guide to the ITT* NC. London and New York: Routledge/Falmer.

Hart, S. (Ed.) (1996) *Differentiation in the Secondary Curriculum: Debates and Dilemmas*. London: Routledge.

Heaney, S. (1966) *Death of a Naturalist*. London: Faber and Faber.

Heaney. S. (1980) *Preoccupations: Selected Prose 1968–1978*. London: Faber and Faber.

Henry, J. (2007) "Professor pans 'learning style' teaching method", *The Daily Telegraph* 29 July, http://www.telegraph.co.uk/news/uknews/1558822/Professor-pans-learning-style-teaching-method.html (accessed 12/03/10).

Illeris, K. (2007) *How We Learn: Learning and Non-Learning in school and beyond*. London: Routledge.

Jakobson, R. (1960) 'Closing statement: linguistics and poetics', in T.A. Seboek (Ed.) *Style in Language*. Cambridge, Mass., MIT Press.

Kolb, D. A. (1984) *Experiential learning: experience as the source of learning and development*. Englewood Cliffs NJ: Prentice Hall.

Kolb, D. A. (1999) *The Kolb Learning Style Inventory, Version 3*. Boston, MA: Hay Group.

Kolb, D. A. (2000) *Facilitator's guide to learning*. Boston, MA: Hay/McBer.

Krathwohl, D. (2002) 'A Revision of Bloom's Taxonomy: An Overview', *Theory into Practice* 41, 4, 212–218.

Kress, G. (1995) *Writing the Future*. Sheffield: National Association for the Teaching of English.

Kuhn, H. W. (Ed.) *Classics in Game Theory.* Princeton, NJ: Princeton University Press.

Kutnick, P. and Rodgers, C. (eds) (1994) *Groups in Schools.* London: Cassell.

Landy, F. J. (2005) 'Some historical and scientific issues related to research on emotional intelligence', *Journal of Organizational Behavior, 26,* 411–424.

Locke, E. A. (2005) 'Why emotional intelligence is an invalid concept', *Journal of Organizational Behavior, 26,* 425–431.

Macey, D. (2001) *Dictionary of Critical Theory.* London: Penguin Books.

Maslow, A. H. (1954) *Motivation and Personality.* New York: Harper & Row.

Marshall, B. (2000) *English teachers: the unofficial guide: researching the philosophies of English teachers.* London: Routledge.

Mayer, J. D. & Salovey, P. (1993) 'The intelligence of emotional intelligence', *Intelligence, 17,* 433–442.

McGregor, D. (2007) *Developing Thinking; Developing Learning: A Guide to Thinking Skills in Education.* Maidenhead: OUP /McGraw-Hill Education.

McGuinn, N. (2001) 'Finding a voice through email: a report on two English secondary school email projects', in W. Frindte, T. Köhler, P. Marquet and E. Nissen (eds) *Internet-based teaching and learning (IN TELE) 99,* Frankfurt am Main: Peter Lang.

McGuinness, C. (1999) *From Thinking Skills to Thinking Classrooms: a review and evaluation of approaches for developing pupils' thinking.* London: DFEE Research Report RR115, Norwich: HMSO.

Morrison, K. (2001) 'Jürgen Habermas', in J.A. Palmer (ed.) *Fifty Modern Thinkers on Education.* London and New York: Routledge.

Mortiboys, A. (2005) *Teaching With Emotional Intelligence: A step-by-step guide for higher and further education professionals.* London and New York: Routledge.

Mosley. D., Baumfield, V., Elliott, J., Gregson, M., Higgins, S., Lin, M., Miller, J., Newton, D., Robson, S. (2004) *Thinking skill frameworks for post-16 learners: an evaluation. A research report for the Learning and Skills Research Centre.* Guildford: Learning and Skills Research Centre.

Murray, J. H. (1997) *Hamlet on the Holodeck: The Future of Narrative in Cyberspace.* Cambridge Massachusetts: The MIT Press.

Neelands, J. (1984) *Making Sense of Drama.* Oxford: Heinemann.

O'Driscoll, D. (2008) *Stepping Stones: Interviews with Seamus Heaney.* London: Faber & Faber.

OFSTED (2003) *Yes he can: Schools where boys write well.* Ofsted Publications Centre.

OFSTED (2009) *English at the crossroads: An evaluation of English in primary and secondary schools, 2005/08* http://www.ofsted.gov.uk/publications/ 080247 (accessed 05/10/09).

Onyett, N. (2008) 'Creating Texts: Transformational Writing in A-Level English Literature', *The English Review* 19, 2, 13–16.

Orme, G. (2001) *Emotionally Intelligent Living.* Carmarthen: Crown House.

Perkins, D. (1995) *Outsmarting IQ: The Emerging Science of Learnable Intelligence.* New York: The Free Press.

Petty, G. (2006) *Evidence Based Teaching: A Practical Approach.* Cheltenham: Nelson Thornes.

QCDA (2010) *Personal, learning and thinking skills* http://curriculum.qcda.gov.uk/key-stages-3-and-4/skills/plts/ (accessed 16/010/10).

Reed, E. S. (1996) *Encountering the World: Toward an Ecological Psychology.* New York: Oxford University Press.

Revell, P. (2005) 'Each to their own. The Government espouses the theory of learning styles with scant regard to the evidence', *The Guardian,* 31 May.

Rogers, C. (1983) *Freedom to Learn for the 80's.* Columbus, OH: Charles Merrill.

Rogers, C. R. (1951) *Client-centred Therapy: Its Current Practice, Implications and Theory.* Boston: Houghton Mifflin.

Rosenblatt, L. (1970) *Literature as Exploration.* London: Heinemann.

Sage, L. (2000) *Bad Blood.* London: Fourth Estate.

Salovey, P. and Mayer, J. (1997) 'What is Emotional Intelligence?', in P. Salovey and D. Sluyter (eds) *Emotional Development and Emotional Intelligence: Implications for Educators.* New York: Basic Books.

Sampson, G. (1925) *English for the English.* Cambridge: University Press.

Simon, B. (1985) 'Imposing differentiation in schools', *Education Today and Tomorrow,* 37, 3, 4–5.

Sluyter (eds) *Emotional Development and Emotional Intelligence: Implications for Educators.* New York: Basic Books.

Smagorinsky, P. (2002) 'Growth Through English Revisited', *The English Journal,* 91, 6, 23–29.

Smith, E. (2009) *The Great Western Beach: A Memoir of a Cornish Childhood Between the Wars.* London: Bloomsbury.

Steiner, C. and Perry, P. (1997) *Achieving Emotional Literacy.* London: Bloomsbury.

Sternberg, R. (1985) 'Towards a triarchic theory of human intelligence', *Behavioural and Brain Sciences,* 7, 269–87.

Swift, G. (1992) *Waterland.* Basingstoke and Oxford: Picador.

Terr, L. (1990) *Too Scared to Cry.* New York: HarperCollins.

Terry, P. R. (1997) 'Habermas and Education: knowledge, communication, discourse', *Curriculum Studies,* 5, 3, 269–279.

Thurgar-Dawson, C. (2008) 'Transformative Writing: Re-creating the Literary Text', *E Magazine* 41, 25–26.

Tomlinson, C. A. and McTighe, J. (2006) *Integrating Differentiated Instruction and Understanding by Design: Connecting Content and Kids.* Alexandria, VA: Association for Supervision & Curriculum Development.

Twist, L., Schagen, I. and Hodgson, C. (2007) *Readers and Reading: the National Report for England 2006* (PIRLS: Progress in International Reading Literacy Study). Slough: NFER.

Vygotsky, L. (1986) *Thought and Language.* Cambridge, Massachusetts and London, England: The MIT Press.

Weston, P., Taylor, M., Lewis, G. and MacDonald, A. (1998) *Learning from Differentiation: A review of practice in primary and secondary schools.* Slough: NFER.

Wilkinson, A., Barnsley, G., Hanna, P. and Swan, M. (1980) *Assessing Language Development.* Oxford: University Press.

Younger, M. and Worthington, M. (2005) *Raising Boys' Achievement: a study funded by the Department for Education and Skills.* Norwich: HMSO.

Index

Page numbers in **bold** denote figures.